THE CRASH OF MH370

Recently Retired A380 Airline Captain
Explores the Mystery of the Doomed Airliner

By

James Nixon

CrammondMEDIA

ISBN: 978-0-9944760-3-6
(paperback)

The Crash of MH370

An Excellent Read

Mick Rooney – Aviation Journalist
(Five Star Amazon Review)

"In **The Crash of MH370**, James Nixon has concisely and factually examined the greatest aviation mystery, bringing to bear more than 30 years as a pilot flying some of the most advanced and technical passenger aircraft ever built. When you want an expert opinion you ask someone with the experience of sitting on the flight deck for a living and someone who understands the technical and human aspects facing pilots today.

Far too many books have been written about MH370 by well-meaning overnight armchair experts, and conspiracy theorists looking to sow the seeds of their latest political, cultural hang-ups, and fantasy plots for the next Tom Clancy novel. As an aviation journalist, I've read my share of books penned by people who woke up one Saturday morning in 2014 and magically knew the difference between an APU and an SUV.

From the outset of this book, Nixon reminds his readers that the simplest explanation to an air crash is often the one closest to the truth and that there is always the danger to attribute what we don't understand to the nefarious or elaborate theories and scenarios.

Working through a number of theories, he presents his own opinion and theory on MH370 and 13 recommendations the industry should examine and implement.

An excellent read if you really want to cut through the misinformation and BS written about MH370.

Let's search on. The aviation industry needs it, and the flying public; but there are also 239 souls who deserve it at the very least."

Mick Rooney – Aviation Journalist
www.**MH370investigation**.com

****

Read 65 reviews at the book's website
www.TheCrashOfMH370.com/**ReaderReviews**/

Amazon.com has 60 reviews
Average rating 4.7 / 5 stars
Go to Amazon.com and search MH370

A Gripping Page-Turner
WRR (Amazon Customer) 5 Stars

The author describes the facts of the MH370 tragedy from the perspective of a subject matter expert, a recently retired large passenger jet captain. Along the way the reader is treated to frequent glimpses of the vast fund of knowledge these aviators have to maintain delivered in straightforward language. Extremely well written!

****

Credible and commendable. You will indeed "learn stuff you've never heard before"
Anonymous (Amazon Customer) 5 stars

As a former Airline pilot and Air Traffic Controller, I now read most MH370 analysis with skepticism. For the first time, I've found a review of the facts that raises no eyebrows. Don't mistake that for a book that is uninteresting - it's quite the opposite; in fact, this is the best aviation book I have read in several years. When James tells us "Stick around; you're going to learn stuff you've never heard before", he's not kidding. There are countless gems of wisdom in here that every pilot and controller will find fascinating, and also, very useful in practical application. His theory of the reason for the incident is the most credible I've read. And his exoneration of the two pilots on this flight is not only justified, but highly commendable. James, thank you for writing this book.

The Crash of MH370

First published by
CrammondMEDIA in 2017

Copyright ©CrammondMEDIA2017

The moral right of the author has been asserted.

All rights reserved. No part of this book may be reproduced or transmitted by any person or entity, including internet search engines or retailers, in any form or by any means, electronic or mechanical, including photocopying (except under the statutory exceptions provisions of the Australian *Copyright Act 1968*), recording, scanning, or by any information storage and retrieval system without the prior written permission of the principal of CrammondMEDIA.

National Library of Australia
Cataloguing-in-Publication entry

Creator: **Nixon, James**, 1959- author.
Title: **The crash of MH370** : recently retired A380 airline captain explores the mystery of the doomed airliner / James Nixon.
ISBN: 978-0-9944760-3-6 (paperback)
Notes: Includes bibliographical references and index.
Subjects: Malaysia Airlines Flight 370 Incident, 2014.
Aircraft accidents--Indian Ocean.
Aircraft accidents--Investigation--Indian Ocean.
Search and rescue operations--Indian Ocean.
Aeronautics--Safety measures.

Amazon: https://www.amazon.com/dp/B06WLHKNMX

Website: www.TheCrashOfMH370.com

Updated: 15th June 2017

LEGAL DISCLAIMER

The views expressed by the Author are his own. The information provided within this book is for general informational purposes only. While we try to keep the information correct, there are no representations or warranties, express or implied, about the completeness, accuracy, reliability, suitability or availability with respect to the information, products, services, contained in this book for any purpose. Any use of this information is at your own risk.

Various paragraphs in this book have used information from the official investigation sources, articles appearing on both the internet and in the media. Correct attribution and links to the source material are given. If you can find any paragraph where correct attribution has not been given, advise us, and we will make amendments to subsequent editions.

The author, his agent and publisher do not have any control, warrant the performance, effectiveness or applicability of sites listed or linked-to in this book or use by any third party of this book's content, through any physical or electronic medium or of such third party's content and opinion. All links and references in this book are for information purposes only and are not warranted for content, accuracy or other implied or explicit purpose.

While the author has made every effort to ensure that the information in this book was correct at the time of publication, neither the author, his agent nor the publisher assume any responsibility for errors, or for changes that occur after publication.

The Author, its agent and publisher, to the fullest extent permitted by law hereby disclaim any liability to any party for any expense, loss, damage, physical or mental anguish or disruption caused by the statements, opinion, errors or omissions, whether such errors or omissions result from negligence, accident, or any other cause.

No part of this book may be reproduced or transmitted in any form or by any means, electronic or mechanical, including photocopying, recording or by any information storage and retrieval system, without written permission from the author. Direct all enquiries to:
kerryn@CrammondMedia.com

©CrammondMEDIA2017

TABLE OF CONTENTS

The Known Facts	1
The Players	12
The Pilots	21
The Flight	27
Losing Contact	34
The Search	47
Theories	60
Bomb /Explosive Decompression	62
Accidental Shootdown	63
Mid Air Collision	64
Hijack / Hypoxia	66
Loss Of Control – Inflight	76
Suicide	80
Multiple Failures	83
Lithium Battery Fire	90
My Analysis	96
Conclusions	124
Recommendations	126
What's Next?	142
Acknowledgements	144
Additional Viewing / Reading	146
Appendix	147
List Of Abbreviations	148
Glossary Of Terms	153
The Website	158
Also by James Nixon	159
Endnotes	162

The Crash of MH370

DEDICATION

In Memory
of
Steve Ashton

***

Dedicated to
The passengers and crew
of MH370

Their families, friends
& colleagues

The investigators

The searchers

&

Everyone who has turned their
mind to helping solve
the mystery of
MH370

The Crash of MH370

FOREWORD

So, what makes me qualified to talk about the matter?

With over 31 years flying experience, I have worked as a pilot for airlines in Australia, Malta, the United Kingdom, Vietnam, Bahrain, and the United Arab Emirates, and flown extensively all over the world, except for Central and South America. In late 2016, I took early retirement from my role as an A380 captain. Previously a captain on the A330, I've also flown the Boeing 727, Airbus A320, A321, A330, A340 and A380 as a first officer and have clocked up nearly 18,000 hours.

As a pilot with Ansett Australia, I was active on the company's safety committee, and on various management projects. I also co-edited the airline's Airbus fleet newsletter, "The Bird."

In 2000, I was awarded both the Aviation Safety Foundation of Australia's Air Safety Award and the Aircraft Owners & Pilots Association President's Award, after successfully talking-down, from our A320 circling above, three pilots lost in heavy weather over Kangaroo Valley.

I've long combined my passion of flying with that of writing and photography. (Though, after they banned pilots worldwide from taking photos from the cockpit —supposedly for your safety— I started planning my retirement.)

Some of my previous works include the Kindle bestseller, *Sleeping For Pilots & Cabin Crew (And Other Insomniacs)*, as well as *On Tour: Travels With An Airline Pilot*, and ... *And That's My Side Of The Story*.

The Crash of MH370 has been reviewed by a small team of industry professionals including five Boeing 777 captains; an Airbus acceptance test pilot now flying the Boeing 787; a director of flight operations with a wealth of experience flying the Boeing 767, 737, 727, Fokker 28, corporate jets and commuter airplanes; and an aeronautical engineer, among others.

All agree on the importance of the issues I have raised. One of our group noted:

"This may well be one of those ground breaking accidents that changes our thinking."

Every now and then there is a crash that changes the industry. The Manchester crash, from which came fire-blocked cabin interiors; the Kegworth crash, which gave us Crew Resource Management (CRM); Lockerbie, which changed our minds about security and the way passenger bags are handled; and from Mt. Erebus, we discovered the whiteout phenomenon and changed the way we do navigation. In flight-training classrooms the world over, just like yelling out the punch line to an old (but good) joke, all you have to do is say the name of the crash and everyone is on the same page. From the "Gimli Glider" to "Swissair 111," the code names can quiet a rowdy room as we all think: *"There, but for the grace of God, go I."*

Every airline pilot studies the 20 or so ground-breaking investigations, and files the important facts into their mental toolbox. Facts which shape their work personality and are referred to every flight. MH370 is one of those crashes.

Already MH370 has changed two things: all flight recorders now have to have battery power for 90 days instead of 30; and from 2018, airliners will have to transmit their position every 15 minutes.

Throughout the text you will notice that I have used the pronoun 'he' when referring to pilots. This is simply for ease of reading. The world is now, thankfully, populated by female pilots. And it is a much better place for it. Captain Hollie Burroughs has taken my seat in the A380. It couldn't go to a better flier.

The Crash of MH370

INTRODUCTION

My sister asked me to write this book.

"You need to hurry," she pleaded; "I could be Captain Shah's sister. That could be me."

She was right, and Captain Shah could be *me*.

Every time someone denigrates Captain Zaharie Shah and First Officer (FO) Fariq Hamid, they are turning a red-hot poker in the guts of their families, colleagues and friends. And most pilots. The loss of MH370 launched a 24-hour media cycle in which the only participants were the non-aviation journalists interviewing each other and a group of "experts" who appeared to have little idea what they were talking about.

We call these interviewees "rent-a-mouths," in much the same way people who sit at the end of runways watching airplanes are called "anoraks." If you had ever flown a light plane (or been in a big one), you could've grabbed a spot in the limelight—and many did. From where we sat in our cockpits, it seemed that the only people who *weren't* interviewed were those who knew anything about doing the job.

Admittedly, one retired 777 pilot briefly held the floor, completely convinced that Captain Zaharie Shah killed everyone and then made his aircraft vanish. Some trick. Australia's crash investigators have since discredited his claims on two separate occasions. But for most big-jet pilots, constrained as we are by our confidentiality contracts, all we could do was sit and watch, gob-smacked, as the sideshow continued without us.

Simply put, most of the people you have been listening to about this crash are not experienced long-haul, jet-airline transport pilots. Some have flown "toy airplanes," as we call them; most are mainstream journos or interested parties. Then there are others, well meaning conspiracy theorists, who act like they smoke way too much dope before emailing me at 4 am. For some reason the sane, experienced aviation journalists were lost in the noise.

Seriously, if Captain Shah had wanted to send a message to his prime minister for the incarceration of Malaysia's previous deputy prime minister, Anwar Ibrahim, (as some conspiracy theories go), he would have pointed his fuel-laden 777 at the Petronas Towers and said: *"Watch this!"*

Wouldn't you?

The Crash of MH370 has been written on behalf of all the crews who are unable to speak publicly. First it lists the known facts without any thoughts from me. Then we look at the players, the pilots and the organizations involved in the search.

I offer you an understanding of how the aviation world works, and explain what happens when a plane is lost or crashed. Next we'll examine the flight and search in detail, then study various theories surrounding the disappearance, and dispatch them with insider knowledge. I then leave you with my best guess as to MH370's fate, and 13 industry recommendations.

Stick around; you're going to learn stuff you've never heard before.

James Nixon
June 2017

*****

Throughout the text I have adopted the convention of spelling out an item's or organization's full name before adding the abbreviation when first mentioned, then using just the abbreviation thereafter. To help I have included a **List Of Abbreviations** just before the book's glossary on page **148**. To satisfy the global market the text uses American English.

Maps, documents and photos are available on the website:
www.TheCrashOfMH370.com

The Crash of MH370

THE KNOWN FACTS

The industry uses Universal Time Coordinated (UTC), also known as Greenwich Mean Time (GMT); in this chapter, I am using Malaysian local time for ease of understanding.

Friday March 07th, 2014

22:50 – Captain Shah signs on.
23:15 – FO Hamid signs on.
The crew orders 49,100 kilograms (kg) of fuel for the flight, giving an endurance of 7 hours and 31 minutes including reserves. The planned flight duration is 5 hours and 34 minutes. To cover flight to an alternate airport and standard reserves, this fuel figure is normal.

Saturday March 08th, 2014

00:40 – Kuala Lumpur Tower issues takeoff clearance for the Beijing-bound MH370—a Malaysian Airlines (MAS) Boeing 777-200 extended range (ER) airliner registered as 9M-MRO.

00:41 – Within 90 seconds, MH370 departs from runway 32R, Kuala Lumpur International Airport (KLIA), with a total of 239 persons on board (227 passengers and 12 crew), as well as 4,566 kg of mangosteen fruit, 221 kg of lithium batteries (that the Captain does not know are on board), passenger baggage, some incidental freight, and a 6 kg shipment for UPS.

00:42 – After being transferred to Lumpur Departures, air traffic control (ATC) clears it to climb to 18,000 feet (flight level 180) and to track direct to waypoint "Igari," the Flight Information Region (FIR) boundary with Vietnam. Captain Shah makes the radio calls, so we can deduce that FO Hamid is the operating pilot.

00:46 – MH370 is transferred to Lumpur Radar ATC and cleared to climb to 25,000 feet (flight level 250).

00:50 – Captain Shah is given clearance for further climb to their cruise altitude of 35,000 feet (flight level 350).

01:01 – The aircraft reaches top of climb, flight level 350. This is reported by the captain.

01:07 – MH370 is level at flight level 350 and Captain Shah reconfirms his level with ATC. The Aircraft Communications Addressing and Reporting System (ACARS) makes its final contact with MAS Engineering, recording the remaining fuel of 43,800 kg at 35,004 feet altitude.

01:07:48 - 02:03:41 – The satellite communications system fails between these times.

01:11:59 – Ho Chi Minh acquires the aircraft with both its secondary surveillance radar (SSR) and with Automatic Dependent Surveillance – Broadcast (ADS-B).[1]

01:19 – Lumpur Radar ATC hands the flight to Ho Chi Minh ATC as the aircraft approaches waypoint Igari. Despite Captain Shah being the one making radio calls, it's FO Hamid who responds, using typical phraseology:

"Good night Malaysia Three Seven Zero."

It is the last transmission ever heard from the airliner.

01:20:31 – MH370 crosses waypoint Igari.

01:20:36 – Five seconds later, the Mode S transponder return ceases.

01:21:13 – Thirty-seven seconds afterwards, the SSR return vanishes off screens in Malaysia.

Military radar and radar sources from Vietnam and Thailand also capture the disappearance of the radar position symbol of MH370 at about the same time. Ho Chi Minh also loses ADS-B information.

01:21:13 – Malaysian military primary radar shows MH370 has made a fifteen degree course correction from waypoint Igari towards Bitod. Abruptly the 777 makes a constant left turn to a south-westerly direction. Sadly, no humans pay attention to the primary radar signals. This and all the subsequent radar glimpses are recovered after the fact.

New Zealander Michael McKay, a trained observer on the oil rig *Songa Mercur* off Vũng Tàu, Vietnam, sees what he believed to be the plane "burning" at altitude for 10 to 15 seconds. Although McKay claims that "the timing was right," he neglected to include the exact time in his report, which did include sea state, wind direction and speed, as well as bearing and distance to the target. McKay reports the event to his employer and Vietnamese authorities and eventually loses his job for going public. Six months later, on ABC Radio Melbourne, he reveals that no investigators ever contacted him. Eventually he was interviewed by NZ police, who treated him as a credible witness, and subsequently Interpol forwarded his statement to the investigators.[2] However, the position of his oil rig was 306 nautical miles (566 kms) away, well below the visible horizon; and his bearing was out by 10 to 20 degrees. He probably saw a meteor.

01:30 to 01:35 – For five seconds, Malaysian primary radar shows that the Boeing is on heading 231 degrees magnetic, ground speed of 496 knots (kts), and height of 35,700 feet.

01:36 – For 40 seconds, radar shows the heading has turned right six degrees to 237 magnetic, groundspeed fluctuating between 494 and 525 kts and height fluctuating between 31,100 and 33,000 feet.

01:40 – During a momentary primary radar contact the heading is 244 magnetic, ground speed 529 kts and height at 32,800 feet.

01:52 – The radar return is observed to be just south of Penang Island.

The investigation team noted that the position and heading of the primary radar return from both civilian and military radar suggests it was from the same target. The plane must have then performed a right turn of up to 70 degrees to appear at the next point. It was the last radar return to show on KL ATC's primary radar, though the military radar continued to track the blip as it headed towards Pulau Perak, a small island in the middle of the Straits of Malacca, abeam Langkawi.

02:02 – The military's radar return registers over Pulau Perak and tracking continues as the airliner is observed to be heading west-north-west towards waypoint "Mekar," a waypoint on Airway N571.

02:03 – MAS Operations sends an ACARS message (44 minutes after the last radio call), advising the crew to contact Ho Chi Minh radar. The system advises that the message has not been received by the aircraft.

02:22:12 – The radar return disappears abruptly 10 nautical miles (nm) after waypoint Mekar, which is on a rough line between Banda

Aceh and Phuket, closer to Banda Aceh.

02:25 – Data gathered from Inmarsat's Indian Ocean Region (IOR) satellite indicates that the aircraft has continued approximately on that track. This data becomes known as the first "handshake" after a log-in was initiated by the aircraft, maybe after a power interruption to the electrical system. Notably, during the log-on phase the unique flight identifier is not included.

02:40 – A satellite telephone call sent to the aircraft by Malaysian Airlines (which went unanswered), generates Burst Frequency Offset (BFO) data as the call rings. This data shows that the aircraft has turned more than 90 degrees left and is headed south.

By analyzing signals transmitted by the aircraft's satellite communications terminal to Inmarsat's satellite, investigators discovered that the aircraft continued to fly for several hours after loss of contact.

The analysis shows the aircraft had changed course shortly after it passed Indonesia's northern tip and traveled in a southerly direction until it ran out of fuel in the southern Indian Ocean, west of Australia.

When a satellite ground station is logged on to an aircraft, if it has not heard anything for an hour it generates a log-on interrogation message using the aircraft's unique identifier. Upon receipt, the aircraft replies with a short message confirming that it is still connected. This is known as a "handshake." We will discuss how a handshake becomes a position arc later.

02:51 – This is the time, ninety-minutes after the loss of radar contact, is the latest time that an ATC "distress phase" should have been declared. Had it been declared soon after attempts to contact the aircraft failed, the Thai, Indian, and Indonesian controllers may have closely scrutinized primary radar returns and seen something. (MH370 must have flown close to Indonesia's Banda Aceh.)

03:41 – Second handshake initiated by the ground station.

04:41 – Third handshake initiated by the ground station.

05:30 – The KL Aeronautical Rescue Coordination Centre (ARCC) is activated.

05:41 – Fourth handshake initiated by the ground station.

06:32 – Malaysian ATC issues a distress phase (DETRESFA), over three and a half hours later than would be expected by every air traffic controller operating flight crew on the planet.

06:41 – Fifth handshake initiated by the ground station.

07:13 – A second unanswered ground-to-air telephone call.

08:10 – Sixth handshake initiated by the ground station.

Calculated from the fuel-on-board figure transmitted at the final ACARS position, the aircraft was running out of fuel.

Based on historical engineering data, MH370's right engine was using more fuel than the left, so would have flamed out about 15 minutes earlier. When the remaining engine failed, as soon as its electrical generator dropped offline, the ram air turbine (RAT) would have deployed into the airstream and the auxiliary power unit (APU) would have started, and run until it used up its 30 lbs of fuel.

As soon as the APU generator came online, the system performed a system test and "log-in handshake" with the satellite, generating a log-on request. This log-on location is the "7th arc."

08:19:37 – The log-on process is completed.

08:21:06 – The expected log on of the in-flight entertainment (IFE) system does not occur.

The final two SATCOM transmissions from the aircraft at **08:19.29** (log-on request) and **08:19.37** (log-on acknowledge) provide the last factual data related to the position of the aircraft. We can surmise that the crash occurred between **08:19** and **08:21** Malaysian Time.

11:30 – The first search aircraft takes off, flying to MH370's last confirmed location on the Vietnamese border. However, the aircraft is not in the Gulf Of Thailand; it is in the Indian Ocean.

Twenty-three items of debris have washed

ashore in six countries on the western side of the Indian Ocean. Three items have been determined as having come from MH370. Four are "almost certain to have come from MH370" and the remainder is still under investigation.

Goose barnacles attached to some of the debris confirm the time these pieces had taken to drift across the ocean, based on water temperature and gestation period.

Drift analysis has shown that if the plane crashed in the southern end of the "7th arc" items would have drifted to Western Australia. From the northern end, they would have gone to Asia. To go west, they would have to come from a very localized area.

The initial target area was thought to cover a total of 120,000 kilometers—an area that has now been completely searched. Recent modeling discovered that during its last contact with Inmarsat, the aircraft had entered a rapid descent, consistent with the aircraft crashing. This means that the target area is now about 100 kilometers to the north, at most a search area of an additional 25,000 square kilometers.

Descent rates during the last contact fit within a range of 3,800 to 14,600 feet per minute at **08:19:29**, increasing to between 14,200 and 25,000 feet per minute only eight seconds later at **08:19:37**.

This confirms close examination of the

recovered components, which prove that the aircraft was not configured for a controlled landing as many theories suggested, but instead for high-speed flight.

All crash investigation modeling has assumed an autopilot mode was engaged.

Further investigations with Boeing's Engineering Simulator showed how the aircraft would react in this situation. Over numerous replays, each time the aircraft reacting differently, the consensus is that the radius of flight, after the first flameout, would not be more than 40 nm and more likely 15 nm in a high-speed descent scenario.

Since investigators were now looking for an aircraft that may have gone straight into the ocean, and therefore may bear little resemblance to an aircraft, they used a remote-operated vehicle to re-examine 40 seabed "anomalies."

To ensure they would be able to find the debris, all the scanning equipment used in the search was tested to locate objects measuring 1m x 1m x 2m – the size of a 777 engine without its cowling attached.

As well as mapping the seafloor for the first time, they found the wreck of a sailing ship with all the iron pieces, including the anchor.

The area of the drift analysis is larger than Europe, about the half the size of Australia or the USA.

After concluding the 120,000 square kilometer area the search was postponed indefinitely on the January 17th, 2017.

***

In the above timeline summary, I have quoted extensive slabs from the MH370 Malaysian Investigator's 586-page document entitled "Factual Information - Safety Investigation of MH370",[3] the various reports by the Australian Transport Safety Board,[4] and Michael McKay's email.[5] All are recommended reading. These facts will be discussed in more detail later. To see maps and photos, check out the book's website www.TheCrashOfMH370.com.

THE PLAYERS

The United Nations may not be efficient at keeping peace, but they are excellent when it comes to aviation. Their specialist organization is the International Civil Aviation Organization (ICAO),[6] which sorts out the tangle of the world's airspace, and provides the rules and procedures by which we live, and die. Each country has a regulator who abides by the ICAO rules.

The International Air Transport Association (IATA)[7] keeps the players in line, and arranges how we deal with passengers, cargo, ticketing, and timetables, among other things. IATA proudly states:

> "IATA works with its airline members and the air transport industry as a whole to promote safe, reliable, secure and economical air travel for the benefit of the world's consumers. IATA's 265 member airlines comprise 83% of all air traffic."

I consider ICAO to be like the Formula One's International Automobile Federation (FIA) and IATA to be like Bernie Ecclestone's old Formula One Constructor's Association: One lays down the rules, the other puts on the show. In Australia, IATA members include the major airlines.

If an airline's plane crashes neither of these organizations will hold the investigation. Instead, this is usually carried out by the investigator of the ICAO member country where the crash occurs. In most countries, the investigator is an independent body to the regulator. Important, because sometimes the investigator will make findings against the regulator. For example, in the USA the investigator is the National Transport Safety Board (NTSB) and the regulator is the Federal Aviation Administration (FAA). The findings of any investigation can only be a recommendation, and on more than one occasion the NTSB has asked the FAA to address issues including pilot fatigue, flight medicals, and even the Boeing 787 lithium battery certification process.[8]

When an aircraft registered in one jurisdiction crashes in another country, it's not uncommon for joint investigator status to occur. When UPS Flight 6, a US-registered 747 freighter, crashed in Dubai, the investigators with the UAE's General Civil Aviation Authority (GCAA) worked with the NTSB. Usually the investigators where the crash occurs are the lead investigators. But this isn't always the case. When Malaysia's MH17 was shot down and crashed in the Ukraine, Ukrainian authorities handed over the investigation to the Dutch, whose nationals made up the majority of passengers on board the flight.

In the case of MH370, the Malaysian Ministry of Transport[9] is the investigator, and the Department of Civil Aviation Malaysia (DCA)[10] is the regulator; since there was no proof, initially, that MH370 ever left their airspace the investigation role remained with the Malaysians. Even so, the investigation team consisted of representatives from the US, France, China, Singapore, the UK, Indonesia, and Australia; with Australia being tasked with the specific role of locating underwater wreckage.

Meanwhile, the airline assumes a support role, responsible for looking after the victims' families and their staff, securing all the documentary evidence (paperwork, engineering and crew records, load-sheets, dangerous goods notices to the captain, fuel dockets, flight plans and more), and assisting the investigator in their investigation.

In some cultures, the airline's management will defer to the investigator; they may want to speak to the press but are not allowed to. This often leads the media to accuse the airline of being uncaring, which may not be the case.

The anguish of Malaysia Airlines (MAS)[11] board members was evident when they were finally able to speak publicly about the crash. Prior to this, they had followed protocol and waited for the Ministry of Transport (MOT) to speak first. Maybe the MOT could have handled things better. Thankfully, most countries do not have much experience in crashes and always appear hamfisted as they rush to get their act together; polished media performing is not their normal role.

Australia's role in the MH370 search has been questioned and it's worth explaining who's who in their zoo.

The Civil Aviation Safety Authority (CASA)[12] is the regulator.

Airservices,[13] the government-owned organization that provides the aviation industry with telecommunications, aeronautical data, navigation services and aviation rescue firefighting services for 11 percent of the world's airspace, is in charge of air traffic control.

The crash investigator is the Australian Transport Safety Bureau (ATSB).[14] Its website says that the ATSB is:

> " an independent Commonwealth Government Agency... governed by a Commission and is entirely separate from transport regulators, policy makers and service providers. The ATSB's function is to improve safety and public confidence in the aviation, marine and rail modes of

transport."

Central to this story, and working with the ATSB, is the Australian Maritime Safety Authority (AMSA),[15] whose statutory duty is to provide the national search and rescue service for Australia. Covering 10 percent of the world's surface bordering 10 countries, their beat extends to just south of the Maldives, Sri Lanka and Indonesia, to east of Mauritius.

It's AMSA who looks for you when you get lost in Australia's search area. Ironically, when MH370 went missing, AMSA didn't have an aircraft that could reach all points of their patrol area. That has since been rectified with the purchase of four Bombardier Challenger CL-604 special mission jets.[16]

The ATSB continued to point out:
> "It is the responsibility of the Government of Malaysia, as the state of registration of the aircraft, to establish **why** MH370 disappeared and it has established an Annex 13 Investigation to undertake this activity. All enquiries in regard to the investigation should be directed to:
>
> MH370SafetyInvestigation@mot.gov.my
> Australia was asked by Malaysia to assist in the search effort for missing flight MH370. The ATSB's role is to lead the current underwater search

operations for the missing aircraft."[17]

So, where, underwater, did they look for it?

In their report, "MH370 – Definition of Underwater Search Areas", the ATSB explains:

"Since May 2014, a search strategy group, coordinated by the ATSB, has been working towards defining the most probable position of the aircraft at the time of the last satellite communications at 00:19(UTC). The group brought together satellite and aircraft specialists from the following organisations:

- Air Accidents Investigation Branch (UK)
- Boeing (USA)
- Defence Science and Technology Organisation (Australia)
- Department of Civil Aviation (Malaysia)
- Inmarsat (UK)
- National Transportation Safety Board (USA)
- Thales (UK)."[18]

With the help of the experts, and based on the information provided by Inmarsat data and Boeing's engineering simulator, the ATSB worked out where the plane crashed. There is no doubt that their tracking evidence is valid.

ATSB said the aircraft is in the Indian Ocean; the debris so far uncovered proves they were right. It *is* from MH370 and it came from where they say it should be. If the plane had crashed in any other location along their defined arc, the debris would have drifted elsewhere. This is great news.

Their rigorous search, completed in January 2017, and which covered a localized area of 120,000 square kilometers, failed to find any sign of the plane.

It is difficult to grapple with the immense size of the ocean versus how small MH370's wreckage will be. Despite what you think, a 777 is tiny. You could put 62 of them nose-to-tail along the runways at Dubai, Heathrow, or JFK. Tear a wing off and you could almost hide one in an Olympic-size swimming pool. Crash it straight into the ocean and it may even compress to the size of a bus. Or a minibus.

Another way of looking at it is to take a grain of rice. Cut it in half. Then flick it onto your lounge room carpet and try to find it. If you do manage to find it, then carpet the Melbourne Cricket Ground, Wembley, or Yankee Stadium and get someone to flick it somewhere out there. Then try and find it … from one kilometer up. At night.

You're reading this because you want to know *why* the plane is at the bottom of the sea. Which is at odds with the ATSB, the Australian investigators, who are not interested in *why*, only *where*. You can read the ATSB reports online[19] and marvel at their professionalism. They've even published a book, which explains the science of the satellite position fixing. When they find the wreckage, they'll hand it to the Malaysian investigators whose job is to uncover *why*. To date the Malaysians have done a massive amount of research into *why not*, which has been necessary to help get us towards *why*.

By embarking on the search for *why*, we are doing something that most of the specialized crash investigators are yet to tackle. And we have nothing to work on.

RECAPPING

- A plane gets lost.
- The airline can't speak about it because it is now in the investigator's hands.
- Australia's ATSB has been asked to search underwater for the lost airplane and has coordinated a group of experts to come up with the best guess as to where to look.
- Their best guess is correct, to within a couple of hundred thousand square kilometers in the southern Indian Ocean.
- But it's underwater. Up to six kilometers down.

From The Logbook:

Oceans are huge.

My favorite astronaut, John Young, described NASA's Apollo guidance system for the return to earth from the moon:

"When the guidance system was working we could splashdown within a few miles of the recovery ship in the Pacific Ocean." He paused, a glint in his eye. *"When it wasn't, we could hit ... the Pacific Ocean. Which, when you think about it, is pretty good for government work."*

THE PILOTS

Captain Zaharie Shah was married with three kids, owned three vehicles and two houses, and had one mortgage and a credit card. Malaysian Police went through his life forensically and found nothing out of the ordinary, in spite of what you have read. In the report, you can even see his banking and insurance details.

He had a paragliding accident and back operation seven years earlier but was fully recovered. Ad infinitum, all-important to check, but kind of creepy because we know that if anything happens to us we can expect the same microscopic examination of our lives.

Likewise First Officer Fariq Hamid, who was engaged, still living with his parents, and had two cars.

I am not going to labor the point, but these were two normal people. After examination the investigators determined:

"There were no behavioural signs of social isolation, change in habits or interest, self-neglect, drug or alcohol abuse of the captain, first officer and the cabin crew."

Investigators even went back through the closed circuit television footage at KL airport and compared the mens' gait and demeanor as they moved through the airport – for the captain over his three previous flights; for the FO, just one.

Nothing. Comparing them to previous days, they looked normal before their final flight.

Even so, early in the investigation, all kinds of rumours circulated that suggested pilot wrongdoing. The rumours relating to Shah and the former Deputy Prime Minister Anwar Ibrahim, (Captain Shah is the uncle of Anwar's daughter-in-law),[20] who was sent to jail the day before MH370 vanished, are false. Shah was not at the court case, but at home repairing a bathroom door at the time and was only informed about the verdict by his wife, according to her brother Asuad Khan.[21]

Simulator

It's worth addressing the "simulator in the home" scenario. We are not privy to Captain Shah's home office, but I will describe what it's probably like.

As well as a bookcase full of training and aircraft operational manuals, ring binders of training notes, past flight plans and textbooks, he would have a copy of *Handling The Big Jets* by

D.P. Davies. The most expensive book ever. Every airline pilot has a copy. After being bamboozled by the high-level physics in the other 323 pages there is only one page we all remember (or understand). One sentence, actually:

"When faced with *stalling* a big jet or doing something else … consider the latter."

Not bad advice, and you can successfully complete an entire career by following it.

Because he was an enthusiastic "aviator" and trainer, Captain Shah may have had the actual-size cockpit panel posters which we use to learn the position of the switches. Many pilots have them framed on walls for reference but some have them mounted on balsa wood, heavy cardboard or Corflute, and positioned as in the cockpit. These are a home-study version of the procedural trainers we use at the training center when first learning the cockpit layout for each new airplane type. It saves wasting time in the expensive full-flight simulators because you can use these to memorize the location of each overhead button and switch. I have seen a few of these full-sized trainers in pilots' home offices but preferred to keep my own posters rolled up, only referring to them when needed.

Every pilot since 1990 has Microsoft Flight Simulator on his home computer. Generation Z pilots have been flying these since they were six. As a result, the new cadet pilots' hand/eye coordination is superlative. Their instrument flying, when they start their careers, is better than ours was with 1,000 hours under our belts.

In fact, Flight Simulator is now so advanced that Captain Shah probably used it to run training profiles. He was, after all, an Examiner of Airmen, whose job is devising scenarios to be run in the simulators.

His "home simulator" was a collection of five screens, three displaying the outside view, one each for the front panel and overhead panels. A control yoke, joystick and throttle quadrant.[22] Serious gaming stuff, as owned by hundreds of thousands of pilots and aviation enthusiasts worldwide. Actual numbers are hard to find. But according to Kieron Gillen, in 2007, 270,000 copies were sold in the US alone, and Flight Simulator was rated ninth in the previous year's top 10 selling programs.[23]

Jos Grupping, on his website "Flight Simulator History"[24] says that, in August 2007, Microsoft boasted that they had sold 10 million copies since the game was launched in 1984. It has now been around for 25 years and the current version boasts that it can fly into 24,000 airports.

Being able to share the flying experience online is what attracts many people, all flying different types of aircraft in the same area, kept apart by gamer air traffic controllers. This has to be seen to be believed.[25] One website, FSX

Multiplayer Live,[26] has 46 groups. On the day I looked, there were four live sessions that you could join, all "flying" into different airports around the world.

To pull a flown flight from his computer, extrapolate a heading and say he planned to fly a 777 over the South Pole to McMurdo Base in the Antarctic is insane. (Yes, that's what was suggested in one theory, despite the fact that he would have run out of fuel before he got a third of the way). It's like stopping a simulator while flying the circuit procedure in New York and extrapolating the last heading to suggest that the pilot was flying to Sydney, or London.

Regardless of these theories, his brother-in-law says that the simulator program became corrupted about a year before the crash so Captain Shah had stopped using it, and that his wife wanted him to dismantle it to make space.[27] The US Federal Bureau Of Investigation (FBI), contracted to help, has cleared his computer of foul play. I also discount it as more conspiracy noise. You should too.

RECAPPING

- Both pilots were normal people.
- Investigators have gone through their lives forensically and given them a clean sheet in all aspects.
- Captain Shah used Microsoft's Flight Simulator on his home computer. This is common for hundreds of thousands of pilots, aviation enthusiasts and gamers.
- The FBI searched his computer and declared him clean.

THE FLIGHT

After an uneventful cockpit preparation and taxi-out the captain handed over to the FO, who was the handling pilot. We know this because the voice to Lumpur approach radar (operating as departure control) after takeoff was that of Captain Shah.

Captain Shah was a Type Rating Examiner (TRE) and was conducting the last training flight for FO Hamid, who was converting from the Airbus A330 to the Boeing 777.

Unlike the cabin crew, who can operate on multiple types, pilots can only fly one type of airliner at a time. Hamid had started his career on the MAS 737s, which he flew for over two years before being promoted to the A330 for 15 months.

Four months before the crash flight he started his 777 training, first in the ground school, then in the simulators, and finally line training. The simulators are so realistic nowadays that by the time you step inside a real airplane with passengers you already hold the relevant licenses.

Line training is where you do revenue flights with a captain who is a Type Rating Instructor (TRI). They teach you the route network as well as the tips and tricks of flying a real plane with real passengers.

Most sim sessions are stressful, as you are there to learn how to handle all types of emergencies. It's a great feeling to get out in the real world and realize that the planes are not only reliable but you can also land with all the engines working, and without the passengers screaming.

When the training department is happy with your progress, they make you fly with a TRE (in this case Captain Shah) and, if he is satisfied, he will sign you off. This final procedure completes your training. In most companies, you are still a product of the training department until passing this line release check, after which you are handed to the fleet department. But before fleet accepts you, you must do another line check with another TRE. And only after passing this check are you then "cleared to fly the line," a phrase from the Second World War, which indicated a pilot was able to fly any aircraft parked on the flight line.

The trip after the Beijing leg was to be Hamid's fleet line check. For the MH370 flight he would have been asked to choose which leg he wanted to fly, outbound or inbound. FOs usually take the more interesting outbound leg, leaving the captain to fly back to home base. As operating pilot, Hamid would make all decisions unless overridden for safety issues by the TRE (rare). After they had taxied-out Captain Shah would have relinquished the controls for takeoff to the FO, and become the monitoring pilot, in charge of radio and navigation.

We know that Hamid was sharp; his radio procedures on the ground were impeccable. He'd completed his line training, would be feeling nervous, but would be at the top of his game. After handling emergencies in the sim for weeks, he'd also passed the challenging engineering exam, and memorized the 21 systems and all their glitches. Shah had probably smiled to himself, knowing how nervous his FO would be, though also expecting that he was competent.

For this line release check, Hamid would be waiting for the captain to lay small traps for him the whole way to test his knowledge. So, unlike a fully trained line first officer, it's more than possible that Hamid would have been extra vigilant and the most up-to-date person you would want sitting next to you in a crisis.

Which is maybe why he took the radio call as they went into Vietnamese airspace, even though it was Shah's role to do this, while Hamid was the operating pilot. Conscientious FOs often want to prove they can do everything; they are like eager puppies. As a seasoned captain, you often make no mention of this but it's generally easier if they just do their stuff and let you do yours.

MH370 had flown a normal departure off runway 32 Right, received an ATC shortcut direct to Malaysia's exit waypoint and climbed to 35,000 feet. At this stage, Captain Shah was doing the radio. He was changed to sector control, given climb to flight level 250 and then 350. After six minutes into the cruise something happened that demonstrated to me he was at the top of his game.

At 01:03 Captain Shah reported that he was now maintaining his cruise level, flight 350.[28] Shortly after, another aircraft, identifying itself only as Asia 7092, made its first call to sector control, giving its level as flight level 350 and squawk (transponder) code as 3147. Old hands at the game immediately prick up their ears at this—there is another aircraft flying out there at the same level. Because this other plane gave its squawk code, the chances are it was inbound from the FIR boundary. Captain Shah, knowing he would soon be leaving it, would wonder if they were head-to-head on the airway.

Despite this call, the controller immediately responds with "Asian Express 1089, Radar, say again your squawk." The reply, "Squawk 3147" isn't accompanied by the aircraft's call sign. This is a red flag.

The controller immediately replies: "Express 1089 identified, direct to Nipah, Nipah Three Alfa Arrival Runway Three Two Right, level three five zero." (Translation: After identifying the radar return the ATC has given him direct tracking to the start of a standard arrival to the designated runway, but to maintain FL350.)

In the back of Captain Shah's mind there'd be a nagging doubt that "Asia 7092," who is also at flight level 350, has not been resolved. Even so, what follows are two busy minutes as the controller tries to contact yet another aircraft, Asian Express 1017, over five calls, interrupted with a call each to Cathay 719 and Asian Express 1089. From the transcripts, it is clear that the radio procedures of some of the aircraft are not ICAO standard, indicating fatigue or incompetence. Captain Shah, an Examiner of Airmen, would not have been impressed.

He probably hadn't consciously thought "Asia 7092" was a real threat. After all, his navigation display would show any aircraft capable of hitting him. But seasoned pilots like to build a three-dimensional picture of who is around them, and what they are doing. It's called situational awareness and one of the things TREs like to see. Asian Xpress 1089 just probably called in with the wrong call sign.

So, after a minute and fifteen seconds of radio silence, needlessly, Captain Shah says: "Ehhh... Seven (transcribed, more likely "Malaysian") 370 maintaining level 350." The controller takes a few seconds to respond; he's had a look around his screen before acknowledging: "Malaysian 370." In making the call, Shah achieved two things: done a radio check, since it had become very quiet all of a sudden; and brought the controller's attention to his flight—just in case the guy was fatigued or getting tunnel vision over the Asian Express 1017 exchanges.

At the very second of this transmission the ACARS was sending its final transmission to engineering.

When FO Hamid took the radio call to transfer to Ho Chi Minh Control, it's possible that Shah was in the toilet. But I doubt it. Wise old captains like to be in the cockpit when they change into a new country's FIR. He may have been getting up to go to the bathroom, or coming back, but the speaker volume would have been turned up and he would have monitored the changeover.

Why? Well, sometimes the next FIR's airspace is closed. For instance, if Ho Chi Minh had a radar failure, or other emergency, they may refuse admission to all traffic. In which case, they'd make the following announcement:

"Cleared to take up a hold in your present position, remain outside Ho Chi Minh airspace."

Hearing something like this when you are doing 7 nm (13 km) a minute requires quick action. Even if a captain has experienced this just once in his life, or heard it said to another aircraft, he'd want to be in the seat—not having a leak—

when the FO starts drawing circles in the sky. Because it could get messy. I once heard it done to a military transport plane entering Turkish airspace; the ATC had no record of their flight plan.

Soon after FO Hamid responds to Lumpur control's handover to Ho Chi Minh with "Good night, Malaysia Three Seven Zero," MH370 dropped off secondary surveillance radars (SSR) in KL, Thailand and Vietnam. Ho Chi Minh control also lost their ADS-B display at the same time.

RECAPPING

- First Officer Hamid was the operating pilot.
- Captain Shah was doing the radio.
- Uneventful takeoff and climb to flight level 350.
- ATC gave them direct tracking to the FIR exit point.
- Although not his role, First Officer Hamid did the handover radio call to Ho Chi Minh.
- As they left Malaysian airspace they dropped off secondary surveillance radar in Malaysia, Thailand and Vietnam, and Vietnamese ADS-B.

LOSING CONTACT

In the old days, radar was a powerful radio beam. When aimed at an aircraft the metal was enough to bounce back a return, which then displayed a blip on a screen. This was, and still is, called a primary radar, and it was so powerful that it'd probably sterilize the bull in the paddock where the spinning radar head was located. As powerful as it was, though, the primary radar wouldn't return much information. With many years' experience, some old timers used to be able to scrutinize the way the dots moved to develop further ideas about an aircraft's altitude, rate of descent or climb, or track. But, like the bull, they have long since retired.

The modern way is to have a transponder with a four-digit number, unique to today's flight, in the cockpit. That number is issued along with the airways clearance, which is the ATC version of the flight plan given to the pilots to insert into the airplane's flight management system. ATC accepts the flight plan and sends it down the line to all subsequent air traffic service units, each receiving the expected time of arrival, location, air route, and level information. Once the aircraft takes off, the time is updated so their expected arrival is accurate to within two minutes. (ATC always know we are coming as it gives them an opportunity to send an invoice to the airline for the overflight fees and charges. For quite a few third- and fourth-world countries this is a major source of income.)

The lower-powered secondary surveillance radar (SSR) points at the aircraft, triggering a burst of zeroes and ones in digital form, which are sent back to the radar head. It's confusing, because today secondary radar is now the number one radar. (Primary radar is still used for military purposes and as a backup, but it is rarely used for airline ATC anymore.)

Not only does the airplane send back its unique number, it also sends other information, such as ground speed. The controller merely positions a cursor over the blip on the screen, clicks a mouse, and reads these different "tags," including which altitude we have selected. They can also see the plane's predicted path on the radar.

When the approach controller in Heathrow tells you to maintain 180 knots on approach and you chicken out, slowing to 170 knots, she will yell:

"[Callsign] ... I said 180 knots!"

(Well, she did to me). They see all.

Or nothing.

Which is what the modern-day controllers saw when the transponder went out in MH370. Nothing. The primary return was there, still seen by KL ATC's radar in Kota Bharu primary radar station as well as the Malaysian military radar. At 01:30 on a Saturday morning, with no state of alert having been declared, you can understand that the controllers, both civil and military, probably had the primary return's "clutter" (which shows mountains, sometimes rain and large flocks of birds) turned down to make it easier on tired eyes.

It wasn't until the tapes were pulled (an old-fashioned saying; nowadays they'd press buttons) that they had a close look and saw something very weird.

MH370 had made its course correction, fifteen degrees to the right, crossing waypoint Igari and headed towards Bitod at an altitude of 35,000 feet. It then made an abrupt turn to the left onto a south-westerly heading, which would take it towards Penang (where, co-incidentally, Captain Shah was born).

Four and a half minutes later, there is a six-degree adjustment to the right, the altitude drops from 35,000 feet to 31,100 feet, and then back up to 33,000 feet.

We are not talking high-quality radar returns from the primary radar here. These returns came and went, leaving investigators to match up bits of the puzzle.

There was talk that MH370 climbed to 45,000 feet in the sweep of a radar. If it did it must have been taken by a UFO as no 777 can climb 10,000 feet that fast when it is in cruise. Besides, 45,000 feet is above the *certified service ceiling of the airframe (43,100 feet)*, a point where the high-speed and low-speed stall points of the wing intersects. Physics-wise, and at MH370's weight, this was simply not possible.

False aircraft plots happen all the time when aircraft are turning. As the aircraft rolls in a turn, invisible zeros and ones hit the Traffic Collision Avoidance System (TCAS) aerials and suddenly all targets jump left or right. When this happens, it's normal to let the TCAS do a few more sweeps until the targets move back into position with the right tag. And it doesn't take much to register a "4" or "2" rather than a "3" for a few seconds in this digital world.

A Melbourne ATC once confided about the evening a plane lined up on runway 27. As it moved into position, and turned on its transponder, the digital radar tag hitched itself to a passing fuel tanker that must also have had a transponder in it, and the 737 drove up the Sunbury road. The controller had to stop himself looking out the window to see if it was true.

MH370 stayed around 35,000 feet, but the

primary radar is not good at exact altitudes. Later levels indicate 31,100 feet, 33,000 feet and 32,800 feet.

Even GPS isn't foolproof when it comes to altitude. At top of climb it's not uncommon for crews to write down the parameters of all the speeds, levels, thrust-settings and pitch. Then, if they lose all their instruments, they simply reset the airplane back to what it was when all was normal and there is a chance of success.

One way to monitor altitude is to select the GPS screen and look into the data itself and see where it thinks you are. Latitude and longitude are within a few meters. The altitude, when looked down from space, is often out by 1,500 feet. Not that you care. In an emergency, with all your other instruments gone, all you need is a reference point to return to, and to know if you are climbing or descending.

So, as far as I can see from the material released thus far, we don't know what happened to the altitude.

But we can guess.

Radar is line of sight, like very high frequency (VHF) radio. And, like everything in flying, there is a formula for that. You take the square root of your altitude in feet 35,000, (which is 187). Multiply that by 1.23. The answer is in nautical miles, in this case 230 nm.

So, if your radar head was at sea level, and

the aircraft, at 35,000 feet, was going away from you, it'd vanish off your screen when it got to 231 nm (about 425 km). There is an anomaly where, once you have radar contact, it may drag the beam over the curvature of the earth. So aircraft (and radio) going away will remain connected longer than an airplane approaching. But it's no real consequence here.

After turning back from its flight-planned track, MH370 tracked south-west over the Malay Peninsula, towards Penang. It then made a right turn up the Straits of Malacca towards Langkawi (where Hamid had done his pilot training), before its west-nor-westerly heading took it past Langkawi.

Then, at 02:22 Malaysian time, the primary return vanished from the Malaysian military's radars.

But not Inmarsat's satellite. Three minutes later, MH370 performed a log-on handshake, possibly after a power interruption, and the aircraft's direction was unchanged.

Fifteen minutes later, at 02:40, Malaysia operations tried to contact the aircraft by sat-phone. During the time they were trying to establish the call, even though it went unanswered, the returned data showed that MH370 had already turned more than 90 degrees to the left, and was now heading south.

The aircraft's primary "paint" may have been

seen by radar operators in Indonesia, Thailand, and India's Andaman and Nicobar Islands. But at nearing 03:00 on a quiet Saturday morning, with no distress phase activated, you can't blame these operators for not seeing what may have looked like an intermittent flock of birds or thunderstorm return.

That a distress phase had not been declared was sad; some would say negligent. In fact, the confusion between the Malaysian ATC and the Vietnamese is understandable considering one thought he had handed over the aircraft and the other was still waiting to receive it. But it all became a bit confusing for all parties: the actual airspace prior to the Vietnamese border is in the Singaporean FIR, but delegated to the Malaysians.

As an operating pilot, you must update your estimated time of arrival to be within two minutes at every waypoint. After missing a reporting point by three minutes (that is, one minute late), you would expect to be called by the ATC you had been told to contact—in this case, Ho Chi Minh. If ATC tries and fails to contact someone the shorthand term is "no joy." Ho Chi Minh would have called KL back on the landline and said:

"No joy on that MH370, is he still with you?" (Although, since English was not a first language for either, ATC may have used the ICAO standard phraseology: "No contact.")

KL's response would be that he *had* received

a handover reply from the pilot, but he would then broadcast again on their frequency in case of "finger trouble," which exists when the pilots select the wrong frequency, try the new ATC and find no one there, after which they would then return to the previous ATC and say:

"KL, can you confirm the frequency for Ho Chi Minh?"

This sorts out most problems and occurs thousands of times a day throughout the world. It's heartwarming. We know that because we are human, we will make a few errors on each flight. Error trapping is our job and you feel chuffed when you expose one. It's the day you have a flight without trapping a few errors that you should worry. Especially when operating at night, suffering cumulative fatigue.

With nothing heard, both ATCs would call again on their frequencies and, if nothing heard, KL and Ho Chi Minh would ask a nearby aircraft to relay for them.

Failing that, they would try on the emergency frequency 121.5, which is always set up on each plane's second VHF radio set. They would also try to send a CPDLC message (like an sms) if that system had been available, and logged on.

Without a response they would call the airline and ask them to try using ACARS (like an email) or satellite phone to get their pilots to call

ATC.

Pilots going "off-air" is not as rare as you'd think. Most companies require pilots to wear headsets from the time they start taxiing until top of climb. Most turn down the cockpit speakers when they are wearing their "electric hats." If interrupted by, say, a cabin crew entering the flight deck as they are reaching cruise altitude, their routine is broken. They may remove their headsets to talk to the crew, forgetting to turn the speakers up. In which case, ATC or other aircraft calling on their primary and secondary frequencies will go unnoticed.

Giving ATC three minutes to realize the transfer had not been a success, and the fact that they were no longer radar identified by either country, I would have expected an "uncertainty phase" to have been declared by 01:55 local time.

Malaysia's rules require that an uncertainty phase is "A situation wherein doubt exists as to the safety of an aircraft or a marine vessel, and the persons on board." ICAO regulations require this to be done within 30 minutes of the overdue position in a non-radar case.

This upgraded to an "alert phase" when efforts to contact the aircraft by all means possible have failed: "A situation wherein apprehension exists as to the safety of an aircraft or marine vessel and of the persons on board."

Then, one hour after the uncertainty phase

starts, (that is: no later than 90 minutes after it failed to report), if the aircraft is still missing a "distress phase" exists: "A situation wherein there is reasonable certainty that an aircraft and its occupants are threatened by grave and imminent danger or require immediate assistance."

Going by the timeline, the distress phase should have been declared at 02:51. Let's give them until 02:55.

A helpful French air traffic controller has advised me that in a radar-identified case, such as MH370, the time limits do not apply. They can go straight to an alert phase after five minutes and, once they are sure they have lost an aircraft on radar and radio, to the distress phase after ten minutes. Practically it may be difficult to meet these timings, as they may be trying to obtain information from multiple sources.

If it had been declared earlier, radar operators in the neighboring countries would have been alerted and begun asking their air forces to take a close look at primary returns.

The Indonesian ATC may even have been able to see MH370 turning south, flying almost overhead Banda Aceh; but they would not be normally addressed in the Detresfa message. It would go out to countries identified on the actual flight plan. It would have taken some lateral thinking to broaden the initial search area without air force involvement.

Sadly, the distress phase was not declared until 06:32, over three and a half hours later than expected by the average controller or airline pilot. The exchanges that occurred between controllers and the company put the wind up any professional airline pilot who expects that people on the ground are skilled professionals. The misinformation spread by the MAS ops was unbelievable[29] as they led controllers to believe that they were in contact with MH370.

Not only was the distress phase delayed for three and a half hours, it then took a further five hours before a Malaysian search and rescue aircraft took off, heading to the last known position, waypoint Igari on the Ho Chi Minh border.

Sad indeed.

MH370 passed Banda Aceh, turned south and became an interesting conundrum for the boffins working for Inmarsat. Except that it was more than an educational debating point, it was a Boeing 777-200ER that weighed 223.5 tons when it took off, with 239 humans on board.

RECAPPING

- Primary radar is not a patch on secondary radar, but it worked when the aircraft systems turned off.

- The primary radar data was obtained afterwards, when investigators examined recordings.
- After last radio contact, the aircraft made the fifteen degree right turn towards the next waypoint but then abruptly turned left onto a south-westerly heading towards Penang.
- It maintained 35,000 feet and did not commence descent.
- After 4.5 minutes it turned six degrees right and the speed increased a little.
- It descended to 31,000 feet and then climbed back to 33,000 feet.
- Media talk of 45,000 feet was false.
- After Penang it turned right, up the Straits Of Malacca.
- Abeam Langkawi, it vanished off primary radar.
- Soon it logged on to Inmarsat satellite's ground station, still heading west-nor-west.
- It was near the tip of Sumatra, close to Banda Aceh.
- Fifteen minutes later, MAS tried calling by satellite phone. MH370 was now headed south.
- The distress phase should have been

raised by this time.
- Instead, three and a half hours passed before it was raised.
- The first search plane took off five hours later.

THE SEARCH

Satellite

It's hard to believe the cleverness of the investigation's scientists who have been able to make calculations of the interaction between the aircraft and satellite, and their work is worth studying (they even wrote a book about it).[30]

They examined the data from 20 previous flights of this aircraft as it communicated with satellites, then compared the actual tracks flown with their satellite modelling of four of its flights. To develop a control based on the actual evening, they also examined two flights that originated from KLIA at the same time as the crash flight and compared actual tracks with satellite "handshakes" to validate their theories.

Inmarsat's 3-F1 geostationary satellite spends its life on the "Clarke Ring," the place Arthur C.Clarke reckoned a satellite would have to be placed so it appeared stationary above the earth. Launched in April, 1996, its orbit is 24 hours, the same as the earth. At 35,786 km above our planet, wandering around its assigned paddock, 3-F1 is affected by space weather caused by solar flares and the degradation of its orbit. Driven by rocket scientists on earth, they track its movements, both around its assigned paddock and as it goes higher or lower than optimum.

Rocket fuel for its thrusters is finite; when fuel runs out, 3-F1's useful life will end. The people who drive it spend days deciding if they need to intervene, making calculations, and then testing the miniature rocket firings in a simulator before going online and adjusting the position of their expensive baby in space. When a dangerous solar flare or coronal mass ejection causes solar energetic particles to be released from the sun, the rocket scientists can turn the satellite into a safe position to try and protect it from particle damage.

The effectiveness of the solar cells, if damaged, can be reduced by up to 30 percent. On January 20,1994, a solar storm caused Canada's Telesat Anik E2 satellite to suffer damage causing it to spin uncontrollably. Using fuel to stabilize it shortened E2's life considerably.[31]

The meteorologists who produce daily space weather forecasts[32] to be used by airliners operating over the polar regions also provide reports for the rockets scientists of the 1,419 operating satellites, of which 506 are geostationary.[33]

So, it became important to know exactly where Inmarsat's 3-F1 was during MH370's flight. The investigator's experts (and findings) have been challenged by renowned space expert and author, Duncan Steel, in his work with the Independent Group. The IG has been working pro bono, drawing together 15 experts from all over the globe to publicly examine information released by the investigators. Steel's calculated satellite position during MH370's flight is slightly different to that of the official investigators, is probably correct, and may have an impact in determining the exact positions of the arcs.[34]

Arcs

Imagine a cone. The top is where the satellite sits, above the equator at longitude 64.5 degrees east. On the sea surface below, the point is about half way between the Seychelles and the Maldives, 1,100 kms from each location. The same distance towards the south-east lies Diego Garcia, in the British Indian Ocean Territory.

The official investigators, after mind-bending mathematical calculations, could determine a distance from the centre point of the cone for each time that MH370 interacted with the satellite. Somewhere along the cone's position on the planet is where the plane would have been at that time. Each position was called an arc. Further research determined that a Doppler effect existed—the difference in sound that a police siren makes when it passes you—allowing them to decide that the aircraft was in the southern hemisphere.

Seven arcs were calculated and it could be seen from this that the aircraft was headed south. The final arc resulted from an incomplete handshake from the aircraft as it was descending into the sea. Recent modelling has even determined descent rates.

They were correct. The plane ended up in the Indian Ocean. We know that because of the wreckage recovered, the drift modelling and the formation and type of the barnacles attached to the flaperon.

Drifting

Pieces of wreckage made landfall by drifting. Dr. David Griffin, a physical oceanographer with Australia's Commonwealth Scientific and Industrial Research Organisation (CSIRO) has done modelling as part of the Drift Work Group, which also included Asia-Pacific Applied Science Associates (APASA), the US Coastguard, the Bureau of Meteorology (BOM) and Global Environmental Modelling Systems (GEMS).

They calculated the path taken by the first confirmed piece of wreckage, a flaperon from MH370's wing.[35]

Three parts, washed up in LaReunion, Mauritius and Tanzania, are "confirmed as coming from MH370."

There are three pieces of debris "almost certainly from MH370" that washed up on beaches in Mozambique, South Africa and Mauritius.

Four items found in Mozambique, one in Mauritius, seven in Madagascar and two in South Africa are still "under evaluation." One, found in Madagascar is "not identifiable."

In South Africa, what looks to be a piece of the rudder washed up on an unnamed beach on December 23, 2016, and something resembling a flap track fairing washed up at East London beach on January 27, 2017. These items are still to be identified.

So, where in the Indian Ocean is the main wreckage?

By making drift tests, investigators initially narrowed the search area to 120,000 square kilometers, which has now been searched without success.

The drift tests themselves are a work of art, with replicas of the parts being placed at various levels in the water, some affected by wind, others by current, at various locations along the final arc. The drift analysis area is larger than Europe, about the half the size of Australia or the USA.

It turns out that if the airliner crashed towards the southern end of the arc, the debris would have ended up on the Western Australia coastline. Too far north and they would have headed towards Asia. There is a relatively small place on the arc that results in a westward trajectory, to where the pieces were found. Small, of course, is a relative term.

Dr. Griffin's research, with further refinement from the satellite data, has determined that the search area should be moved about 100 km further north on the 7th arc, to a 25,000 square kilometer area at 35 degrees south. In a radio interview with Bob McDonald on Canada's CBC Radio on January 21, 2017, Griffin said he is confident that the search will be resumed at some stage despite being postponed for "political reasons." The seven-minute interview is worth listening to.[36]

To strengthen his position the team obtained an actual Boeing 777 flaperon which they modified to resemble the MH370 wreckage. In the seas off Hobart they confirmed how the flaperon performed with respect to wind and drift. Their latest work was released in April 2017.[37]

The CSIRO research concurs with drift modelling done by the University Of Western Australia.

Barnacles

An IG researcher and MH370 blogger, Richard Godfrey,[38] reports that goose barnacles take a certain number of days to grow to maturity and need the right water temperature to breed; so we can dispel the conspiracy theory that someone tore all the bits off the 777 and scattered them to be found around the beaches of six separate countries. Investigators figured it needed 500 days for the pieces to get to LaReunion. The aircraft's barnacle-covered flaperon was found after 508.

End of flight

The latest news after examining the recovered flaps debris is that they were *not* deployed for landing. Investigators have been back to Boeing's special engineering simulator to run numerous approximations of the "end-of-flight" scenario. This tightened the search area to a radius of 40 nm from the point where the right engine's fuel ran out. At one point they figure it was descending in excess of 12,000 feet per minute (118 kts) although the actual figure may be much greater, up to 25,000 feet per minute (246 kts).

For this, we look at a few cases where airplanes have gone straight in—to buildings, water, mud and earth—at high speed. It's gruesome and the human mind can hardly understand how it works.

Conspiracy theorists find it easier to believe in skullduggery than to believe how a Boeing 757 can go into the side of the Pentagon, making a hole not much bigger than its circumference, folding up the wings and dragging them in with it at 850 kph (458 kts).

It was the same at Colorado Springs, the Everglades and the Musi River near Palembang in southern Sumatra. Hard to imagine that something as large as an airliner can go into the ground, mud and water; in some cases without a trace.

Until we saw the twin towers dissolving before our very eyes most of us had no concept of what happens when you combine physics and gravity.

It's OK to be unable to grasp it. Some things are truly unbelievable.

The investigators have gone back over three types of crashes: 22 loss-of-control crashes; four with cases of unresponsive crew/hypoxia; and four where multiple engine failure/fuel exhaustion resulted in a crash.

For detailed data I suggest we turn to the Challenger space shuttle crash and Swissair 111.

Besides landing Apollo 11's Lunar Excursion Module with less than 30 seconds fuel left, and walking on the moon, arguably Neil Armstrong's greatest work was as vice chairman on the investigation into the Challenger crash. The mammoth report[39] is an exquisite detective story with political pressure, stupidity, sadness, lies and a hero whistle-blower by the name of Roger Boisjoly. The crash culminated in the tank rupture and the shuttle being wrenched sideways at Mach 2, causing the crew compartment to suffer a catastrophic force of up to 20g.

At least three astronauts survived and turned on their personal egress air packs. Since the air packs were not pure oxygen, and although the co-pilot activated some switches to try and restore power, we expect that they were soon unconscious with hypoxia.

Over the next 2 minutes and 45 seconds the crew compartment kept its upward momentum from 45,000 feet until it reached 62,000 feet (18.8 km) before it fell into the sea, experiencing over 200 g-forces when it hit. Physics can be extremely brutal. The crew compartment was doing about 333 kph (18,200 feet per minute /180 kts) and "was severely crushed and fragmented from the extreme impact forces." One member of the search team described it as "largely a pile of rubble with wires protruding from it."[40]

When Swissair 111, an MD11, crashed off Halifax in 1998 it was doing 300 kts (555 kph) but was only 20 degrees nose down, almost inverted. It experienced 300g and disintegrated when it hit the sea. The final report details the recovery of two million items by 350 personnel over 15 months.

Despite the testing conditions they recovered 98 percent of the aircraft, including a slightly lesser percentage of its 250 km (155 miles) of wiring. The ensuing five-year investigation would become Canada's largest and most expensive, teaching us much of what we know about fire and smoke in cockpits.[41]

How far underwater would a 777 go if it was doing the speed of Swissair 111, but pointed straight down? After all, Swissair was flying almost level at 10,000 feet before it started its final descent into the sea. It's conceivable that MH370's fuselage could be compressed into the size of a bus, which, when overwhelmed by pressure, sank like a stone.

The search teams have used resources from Malaysia, Australia and China. Two ships were used to map the unexplored sea floor. Until this event, only 12 percent of Australia's oceans had been mapped. Mapping has revealed, among other things, undersea mountain ranges with valleys four and six kilometers deep.

As well as three ships with towed scanning equipment, teams used a remote operating vehicle to examine anomalies. To ensure reliability, they devised a test area, and demanded that search teams find objects as small as 1 m x 1 m x 2 m. They all did.

Their latest report[42] revealed that sonar scanning discovered 605 level-three sonar contacts, which were assessed as "unlikely to be related to the aircraft"; 39 level-two contacts were assessed as "only possibly being related to the aircraft"; leaving two "high-interest contacts warranting immediate further investigation." These were found to be the iron remains of a timber shipwreck and a scattered rock field.

Seventy-four contacts were investigated and eliminated as being related to MH370.

About 40 of these were revisited after further modeling of the "end-of-flight" scenario revealed that the aircraft was not ditched, but crashed.

The searchers are now in limbo, feeling they have been stopped before reaching the finish line when the finish line is in sight. Dr. Griffin, ever the optimist, believes that eventually they will be allowed to restart the search. When the fuselage wreckage is found, the mission changes from "Where is it?" to "What happened?"

RECAPPING

- The experts were correct. The aircraft is in the Indian Ocean.
- Drift analysis proves that they have chosen the correct section of the final arc for detailed searching.
- The most probable area is 145,000 square kilometers and all but 25,000 square

kilometers has been searched.

- Investigators are sure that they have narrowed down the area to latitude 35 degrees south on the 7th arc. Only 100 kms further north than the area just searched.
- Searching was postponed after the initial 120,000 km^2 target area had been examined.
- Sonar scanning has revealed 646 items of interest; 74 were investigated.
- Forty seabed anomalies were re-investigated.
- Debris, confirmed as having come from MH370, had barnacles attached which could only have grown to that size after being immersed in the sea for a long period.
- Three items, "confirmed as having come from MH370" were found in LaReunion, Mauritius and Tanzania.
- Three were "almost certainly from MH370" and washed up on beaches in Mozambique, South Africa and Mauritius.
- Fourteen pieces, found in Mozambique, Mauritius, Madagascar and South Africa are still "under evaluation."

- Two more pieces found, after the last report was published, in South Africa in Dec 2016 and Jan 2017 are still "under evaluation."
- Examination of the components proves that the aircraft went in at high speed and not in a controlled ditching.
- Scientific analysis of the final transmissions to the satellite from the aircraft show that the aircraft was descending at a very high rate.
- Other crash data, including that of Space Shuttle Challenger and Swissair 111, leads to the conclusion that the debris may be unrecognizable as an airplane.

THEORIES

Many have come up with theories as to what happened to MH370. While some are discounted beyond possibility, eight are worthy of discussion. Before getting to these, I can't help sharing two of the more colorful scenarios that conspiracy theorists have come up with. Some people believe that anywhere that isn't their home country is such a backwater that the residents hide in caves using tin cans and string to communicate. They need to get out more. The cure for ignorance is travel.

Jeff Wise, a science writer,[43] has written about his foray into the media spotlight since he imagined aloud that MH370 was flown to Yubileyniy Airport in Kazakhstan, 30 minutes drive from the Baikonur Cosmodrome. According to Wise, MH370 was stolen by Vladimir Putin. Television station CNN sent a limo to pick him up, and the rest is history. Apparently, a "navigator" told Wise how planes can fly along borders without being spotted.

At night, few pilots can spot a border unless it is lit, like the border between India and Pakistan, (see the book's website for a picture). Anyway, the FIR boundaries are straight lines, often not representative of what is printed on the political map. And, just as they do in the US, all 191 ICAO member states like to make money from overflight rights and are protective about their FIR borders. That's what air forces are for.

Keith Ledgerwood's[44] idea is that MH370 hooked itself behind a passing Singapore 777 and followed it north of India and Afghanistan. He imagines that Captain Shah somehow got hold of the Singaporean flight plan (something even the Singapore captain wouldn't be able to do until a few hours before the flight), met up with it in the sky and shadowed it until he found a country that didn't care much about a military primary radar paint splitting in two.

Ledgerwood fails to understand the workings of the CPDLC, the sms-style communication between the controller and the Singaporean 777, over India ATC's Chennai section of the Bay of Bengal. There is no radio chatter in these areas. Without warning, any plane being followed would climb to another level, receive a direct track and suddenly turn leaving the hapless follower wishing for more speed as the target became a small dot and he became exposed to military radar. Things happen fast in real airliners.

Now to the more credible theories before introducing my own.

1. BOMB / EXPLOSIVE DECOMPRESSION

Bombing was discounted because there was:
(a) No widespread debris field in the Gulf Of Thailand.
(b) No agency or angry nutter taking responsibility for the crash.
(c) The radar information soon became available.

Explosive decompression, and the rapid or emergency descent that follows, is discounted since pilots are skilled at this maneuver (it's quite fun), and it nearly always results in a happy outcome. It takes about four minutes to get down to 10,000 feet when you try and, like the go-around, it's a time we are allowed to have fun chucking the plane around, where safety takes priority over passenger comfort.[45]

Rapid descent is our bread and butter. Pilots can do it with their eyes closed. Because the cockpit may be covered in fog if it's an explosive decompression, some companies will make pilots practice the maneuver with a piece of cardboard bent over the glare shield covering the controls. You reach up and make the adjustments under the cardboard by feel.

First officers hope that the day they do it the captain will be in the toilet, his pants around his ankles, breathing on an oxygen mask. The captain will know he is not needed in the flight deck and won't come out until he hears the PA saying that oxygen is no longer required.

2. ACCIDENTAL SHOOT DOWN

Possible, and the Vietnamese do get trigger-happy, as any hapless pilot who strays over the boarder from Laos near Da Nang will attest. Every day, there are two MiG interceptors sitting on the western runway at Da Nang, ready to scramble. Their mere presence just outside the cockpit window is enough; they haven't shot anyone down … yet.

When I flew for Vietnam Airlines we used to leave Siem Reap, Cambodia, early to get back to Ho Chi Minh City in time for happy hour at the Omni Hotel. We left progressively earlier, flew lower and faster, while Mr Sang the bartender mixed the G&Ts in the executive lounge.

One day, we were told that we were no longer allowed to take off ahead of schedule, as the military didn't want us arriving at their border earlier than planned. Apparently, by arriving early and without warning, someone thought the Cambodians were invading. Not something you want to do to people who own surface-to-air missiles and have been invaded by China (more than once), France, Japan, America and Cambodia.

However, in MH370's situation it was approaching 2:00 a.m. on a Saturday, so there was no training in progress, (air-force personnel like to sleep at nights and have weekends off), and besides, HCMC ATC was expecting them. Despite what you may think, the Vietnamese controllers are excellent.

3. MID-AIR COLLISION

The primary radar trace indicated a turn-back towards the Malay Peninsula. However, there was no other traffic on the night of the crash and no debris field in the area. As with other crashes at altitude, a debris field is huge, with thousands of items that float. We also now know that parts of MH370 have been found in Africa, having been in the Indian Ocean.

The chances of a turn-back with a radio failure caused by one event, then turning into a mid-air with another airliner are infinitesimal, and discounted.

Besides, any other aircraft would have a working Traffic Collision Avoidance System (TCAS) and therefore would have avoided the silent MH370.

Development of TCAS began before 1990

and units are now in every airliner. Monitoring up to 60 targets at a time, the system displays all aircraft that could get within striking distance. If there is a chance the intruder will get within a 45-second force field, the pilots are alerted. If it predicts the intruder will get within 25 seconds one unit becomes "master" and the other "slave." The pilots are given verbal and visual instructions to climb or descend their aircraft. Smart people worked out years ago that turning-to-avoid was inefficient with the inertia of large airliners, compared to a quick wrist movement on the control column or side stick, which would deliver you from danger in a second.

Simply put, TCAS tells you to climb or descend; one plane goes up while the other goes down.

Even if the other guy does the opposite of what the system tells him, (as in the mid-air crash over the southern German town of Überlingen in July 2002), the latest software now issues you with reversal instructions so that you are guaranteed to miss by 300 feet at the time of crossing, which is more than enough.

The maneuver is smooth, doesn't spill the coffee, and is practiced and examined in simulators at least twice a year by every pilot. Often, you have to repeat the exercise as you automatically shallow your descent or climb and the system does not go off. It takes a bit of nerve to keep climbing into the path of another aircraft in an effort to see the system work.

The Big Sky theory adds to your safety: "the sky is so big that you couldn't hit another plane if you tried!" Which is why the best chance of hitting another plane is taxiing around an airport, rather than in the sky. With the 777's wingspan of 61 meters, (an A380's is 79 meters) cockpits are "sterile" (operational chatter only) as we move around on the ground.

So that rules out a mid-air collision, and explains how pilots often witness spurious radar returns on the TCAS displays. As an aircraft rolls into a turn, the TCAS aerials are also rolled. You get "map shift" on your navigation displays displacing the targets. The remedy? Let it settle down.

4. HIJACK / HYPOXIA

In hijacking cases the perpetrators want to tell the world. There has been no such message, life insurance claim, or scribbled lipstick message on a KL airport restroom mirror.

In Australia, hijackings are, more often than not, family court matters and there is always a backstory, which the police are trained to find. No such story was found among the MH370 crew list. Nor among the passengers. While not all had been checked by the time the initial report came out, you can bet they will have been by now. The two Iranian men reported early on in the investigation as traveling on stolen passports, were seeking asylum in Germany.

Fox News' retired US Air Force Lt. General Thomas McInerney claimed that Pakistan wanted to steal a Malaysian 777, despite Pakistan International Airlines already having nine of their own at the time, with three more to come. If nothing else, his interview with Sean Hannity, in which he declared that both MH370's pilots stole the airplane and flew it to Pakistan, (or eastern Iran), made us realize that we never have to waste time watching Fox News ever again.[46]

While Asia's tired controllers managed to miss non-transponder, primary radar paints at 2:00 a.m. (Who wouldn't? Commercial ATC haven't used primary radar for 20 years), the border between India and Pakistan (fenced and lit by India at a cost of USD $100 million) is the second-most volatile border in the world, behind North and South Korea. Along this border they would be using primary and secondary radar, and even infrared.

No one with a current airline transport pilot's license imagines trying to cross into India or Pakistan without calling 10 minutes before the boundary. This is a real industry, governed by the United Nations aviation arm, ICAO, and the operators, IATA. Not Hollywood.

Another conspiracy theory is that MH370 was flown to the Maldives or Diego Garcia. It probably had enough fuel to fly to either. Let's add Colombo, Cocos Island and, at a stretch, Western Australia's Learmonth as well.

I have flown to Male and Colombo at least 20 times. Every airplane that lands is in full view and would be recorded by CCTV, even if the airport workers were all asleep. At Male, someone would notice a 777, since the regular 777 flight, Emirates 656, would need its parking space at 7:50 a.m. Built on reclaimed land, the airport's not a huge place; you need a boat to get to the nearest hotel.

For those who said they saw a white 777 over the islands around the Maldives, they may have been right. Since it's an eco-resort destination, we are not allowed to overfly the islands of the Maldives. Even so, this is also where they breed thunderstorms, and those unstable developing cumulous clouds are best avoided for passenger comfort. So we weave in and around them, sometimes straying over an island (there are 1,200 of them and only 100 resorts so it's worth a risk). A witness may have seen the morning Emirates 777 straying over an island, outside their normal flight path as it prepared for the approach.

The US Air Force base at Diego Garcia is not US territory; it's British and only leased to the Americans. So you would have to get two governments to agree to the hijack and then murder all the passengers and crew.

The 777's weight and tire pressures are such that there are not many landing strips able to support its landing. It's one thing to hijack and divert the aircraft, and even land. But in many places, a 777 would sink into the runway, and melt into the taxiways at hundreds more.

If MH370 parked at Christmas or Cocos Islands, someone would have turned it into a restaurant by now, 'cos it sure would not be flying anywhere soon.

Even the most self-absorbed person would have noticed a 777 parked at a small airport and couldn't have resisted posting a selfie with it. Remember, a photo of the QF32 engine cowling that fell onto the Indonesian school was on Twitter before the aircraft landed back in Singapore.

Besides, if you wanted to add a 777 to your inventory, it's easy to steal a parked airliner without having to deal with the passengers. For one pilot it would take a while, but a few pilots and two engineers could be away in minutes. If you went to Sydney at 3:00 a.m., they wouldn't know you'd gone until it was too late. Name one security guard who is going to drive his car at an airplane doing 200 kph, even if he is protected by an orange flashing light.

Every airport in the monsoon areas of Asia is uphill to the parking stands. The volume of water they need to remove from the ramps during heavy rain is phenomenal. It wouldn't take much to remove an airplane's chocks, release the park brake, and soon she'd be rolling backwards. You'd have the engines started and be off before anyone realized something was amiss.

Airborne, during a flight, it would be difficult to kill all the passengers and crew. You'd be surprised how many people don't want to die. Nelson DeMille's thrilling book *The Lion's Game* has shown how to do it; instead of nerve gas, the conspiracy theorists have Captain Shah depressurizing the aircraft and killing everyone via hypoxia.

There are eight different symptoms of hypoxia. Everyone is born with their own symptoms, which never change. Those of us who have done an Aviation Medicine "decompression chamber run" know our individual symptoms. If we ever note those symptoms airborne we are to grab for our oxygen masks. The industry no longer values such training, as the odds of having to use the knowledge are so small. Most younger pilots have not done the course and don't know their symptoms.

You can't deep breathe your way out of this one; it's to do with air pressure and the alveoli of the lungs. At cruise altitudes the air is thin and the pressure to push the air molecules across the thin alveoli walls is less.

The diaphragm and thoracic cavity forms a negative pressure area and the air coming in from the outside is at a greater pressure.

Up high, that pressure is dramatically reduced and the body has trouble bringing the oxygen from the air into the bloodstream. Supplemental oxygen must be used fast before unconsciousness takes over. Even before then, you can still be conscious, but useless and incapable of saving yourself.[47]

For this, there is a "time of useful consciousness" for each altitude. You must get your mask on before that time runs out. At 35,000 feet it's 30-60 seconds, less for smokers, older passengers and the sick.

The 777's cabin altitude during cruise is between 5,000 and 7,100 feet.

The important numbers are these: the highest cabin altitude the aircrew can legally experience is 10,000 feet. Above that, they need supplemental oxygen. The passengers don't need oxygen until 14,000 feet.

After a depressurization and rapid descent you might notice that although the PA has announced that passengers are allowed to remove their masks, the cabin crew will be walking around with bottles strapped across their chests and breathing oxygen. That's because you are below 14,000 feet and they can't remove them until the cabin is back to 10,000 feet.

Hypoxia can sneak up on you, as it did to the Helios Airways 737,[48] which took off with the pressurization left in manual selection. Golfer Payne Stewart died in a similar crash in the USA, and some mine workers from Western Australia also died in a "ghost plane" that flew all the way to northern Queensland before it ran out of fuel and crashed.

But it doesn't happen like that in a modern airliner.

As the cabin altitude climbs, there are cockpit alarms to attract the pilots' attention. At 11,000 feet, the 777's "cabin limiting valve" closes the two pressurization outflow valves to protect itself.

The "rubber jungle" is set at 13,800 feet. You can launch it manually (and do so for back-up during a rapid descent for pressurization if the cabin altitude is above 14,000 feet) but it is going to deploy all the masks in the cabin automatically by the time 13,800 feet is reached. That's quite a sight.[49]

To differing extents, and with the cabin crew having access to 15 supplementary bottles of oxygen, which will last them hours, and with an "oxygen mask release tool" hidden at every crew position to get all the cabin masks down, you'd have to work hard to kill off the angry passengers if you tried to depressurize the cabin.

To understand what is happening with cabin

pressurization, imagine that the fuselage is a bottle. More air is pumped into the cabin via the engines than is let out from the outflow valves. So the air pressure inside is greater than outside. The higher you go the more the difference between the highly pressurized inside is compared to the outside. You can regulate both the amount of air pumped in and the amount going out the outflow valves.

These new aircraft are well built. There are few holes in the fuselage where wires and cables go through to unpressurized areas, so even if you turn off the air-conditioning (and stop pumping in air) the cabin doesn't do an explosive depressurization. Even if you shoot a hole in a window, it won't do it. The system senses a higher discharge rate than normal, so to maintain the required value it closes the outflow valves a little and the aircraft remains pressurized. The window becomes the outflow valve. You wouldn't want to be sitting next to it, though. It would be chaotic until the system settled down, and a few things like napkins, papers, and maybe even a human may try to get out the hole. Always wear your seat belt.

When the air-conditioning is turned off, the cabin altitude starts climbing, as no air is being pumped in and what's inside the cabin starts leaking out all the small holes where wires and pipes go through to unpressurized areas. There is a maximum allowable rate—say, 500 feet per minute—which is seen by all airline acceptance test pilots, as it is one of the checks you do when purchasing a new plane. You wouldn't want to sign for a new aircraft that had a leaky fuselage; your boss would not be happy.

I cannot find the specified requirement for the 777, but, as an indication, I did a test flight with one Airbus acceptance flight test pilot who told me that new A380 cabins climb at only 200-300 feet per minute when the pressurization is turned off at maximum cruise level. Another Airbus test pilot told me of an old A320, with 58,000 hours on the clock, achieving a cabin climb rate of only 500 feet per minute after the air-conditioning was turned off at max cruise altitude. It had done 40,000 take offs and landings. The 777 would be similar.

In cruise, with 6,000 feet cabin altitude set, if someone shuts off the air-conditioning the plane's interior cabin pressure will start climbing towards 13,800 feet at, say, 500 feet per minute. Fifteen and a half minutes later, as the cabin altitude rises through 13,800 feet the rubber jungle auto-deploys, and you can't turn it off.

If you tried it maliciously, the most up-to-speed FO in the company is going to stop you, even by touching a button and using the code phrase over the PA in the cabin, (No, I am not telling you what it is). Within seconds, the trolleys are being secured, cabin crew are at their stations, and the purser is by your side.

Passenger masks are not attached to bottles like previous airliners or the cockpit oxygen system; they use oxygen generators in the overhead passenger service units. The rubber jungle deployment only releases the latches. Oxygen doesn't flow until you pull the mask down to begin the chemical reaction in the canister above.

Every second row has an extra mask for babies and for the cabin crew and passengers caught standing in the aisle.

With a half-full airplane, you'd have, maybe, four masks in your seat alone. You'd use one until your symptoms started and you'd grab another. Each oxygen generator goes for 22 minutes, so you have over an hour, and that's before you go hunting for other empty rows or medical oxygen bottles, of which there were 15 in MH370.

So, even after the captain thought he had killed everyone, he would run out of the cockpit only to find the huge guy, the SAS soldier on holidays (there's one on every flight), or passengering aircrew from any number of airlines using staff travel, with 12 hours of oxygen bottles, waiting for him to step out of the flight deck. And they would be angry.

But not as angry as the purser.

Nice conspiracy theory, but way too many variables.

5. OVERSPEED, STALL & SPIN: LOSS OF CONTROL

Regardless of what stopped the ACARS and transponder, to not get a word out is very disconcerting. There are few things that can shut pilots up other than having to suddenly fly the airplane in the cruise without autopilot. That's why manufacturers make it so you don't have to.

The air is thin, molecules are a long way apart at 35,000 feet, yet the autopilot is happy to make the calculations and adjustments about 20 times per second. When humans take over it can get rough.

A rising or lowering of the ambient temperature as the plane moves into a warmer or cooler air mass, or a violent wind change as it passes in or out of a jet stream, can cause the aircraft to over- or under-speed. (There was no jet stream forecast in MH370's location.)

Under-speed is not much of an issue, as the aircraft rarely flies at a low speed to start with. So, as the speed starts reducing, the auto-throttle increases to counter the speed wash-off. Over a few seconds, the speed is restored.

In flying, however, often the inertia causes the reverse to happen. The building speed causes an over-speed.

Engine thrust comes off; the speed starts to decay, and so on. On bad days, if it continues—

power off, power on, power off—with turbulence and a wind shift, it may be prudent to disconnect the auto-throttle and manually set the thrust based on that cruise power figure (you wrote down at top of climb), putting up with minor speed fluctuations until it settles down.

The worst-case scenario is when you are at the highest level the plane can safely fly (we call this "coffin corner"). The low-speed stall is not far from your cruise speed, and the high-speed stall is not far either. There will be no reading the paper when you are at this level until the fuel burns off, creating a higher maximum altitude and greater margins.

You would only go that high so early in the flight if you were concerned about getting your planned level due to traffic, or if the level you wanted was already taken and ATC gave you the option of staying low, using up more fuel, or going up straight away. Or, maybe ATC has crossing traffic in half an hour and wants to get you up well in advance, or because they want to go to the bathroom, change shift or go out for a smoke. But this did not happen with MH370. We know this because we have all the ATC transcripts.[50]

So, imagine you are sitting there at 35,000 feet, and the captain goes to the bathroom. (Since the Germanwings crash, a cabin crew member now has to come into the flight deck while he is away, but this rule was enforced more than a year after

MH370 went missing). You are flying in coffin corner, close to maximum speed, and are meant to be calling Ho Chi Minh. It's very dark outside and you are alone.

Boeing's distinctive over-speed warning sounds. There is a lurch, then immediately moderate turbulence. You scramble to reach the seat belt sign and turn it on; the turbulence is nearly severe (definition: "momentary loss off control").[51] The clacker noise doesn't stop and the airspeed zooms ahead, well into the red band on the primary flight display. You scramble to move your seat forward from the relaxed position.

Despite both Boeing and Airbus having excellent autopilot recovery for high-speed excursions (cancel the alarm and watch the aircraft start to climb to wash off speed), frightened pilots have been known to instinctively disconnect the autopilot and pitch-up to slow the aircraft, with no concept of how gentle you have to be at 35,000 feet.

You've never hand-flown an airplane this high up, and it feels like a ham-fisted, muscle-bound dockworker has wrenched the control column full back.

If you had time to notice, in the last few seconds the outside air temperature has gone up 10 degrees as you have flown into a pool of warm air; in an instant the optimum level is 5,000 feet below you, and you're now 2,000 feet above the maximum level for this weight and temperature. Test pilot territory. But you are oblivious to those figures. Hanging on takes your entire concentration. Your head is hot; sweat explodes from every pore. You are scared shitless and it seems that the over-speed warning stopped an hour ago.

All that work on the control column has had its effect on the speed; it is dropping like someone turned off the instrument. You roughly push forward but it's too late: the stall warning sounds and you feel a jolt of the stick-shaker. There is a sick feeling in your bum, the plane is moving in a way you've never felt before; it is trying to tell you something.

The fix in an airliner with underslung engines is to close the thrust levers, level the wings, and lower the nose. Make sure the speed brake is stowed and go for a stage of flap if you are low to the ground. When you are out of the stall, put the nose on the horizon and carefully add thrust, watching for signs of the secondary stall. You'll have lost 3,000 feet; make the pitch no more than five degrees up and put the throttles back to cruise thrust.

If you get into a spin, watch the instruments. Center the control column, push forward a tad. Work out which way the spin is going, then gingerly press the opposite rudder. The spin slows and stops. Now, get it out of the dive you are in.

But you don't do any of that.

Somehow you held it in the stall and there was a shuddering flick of some sort. Did it roll? The artificial horizon makes no sense; is that "up"? It's so dark outside, if only there was a moon tonight.

In the toilet, the captain is pinned to the wall as if in The Rotor at Coney Island. The cabin looks like a bomb has gone off. There is a baby in the overhead compartment and a galley trolley jammed between the wall and a seat, with legs sticking out under it. Lots of screaming.

The large jet is spinning in the darkness, the g-force tears off the right engine and a molten line of flaming gold momentarily joins the two diverging structures until the black resumes again.

There was no debris, and we know that the aircraft turned back. Then Inmarsat's data proved correct, she flew to the Indian Ocean and crashed there.

So, it wasn't over-speed, stall, spin, crash or, as the investigators say, loss of control in-flight (LOC-I).

6. SUICIDE

Until the Germanwings crash,[52] I had omitted mention of the possible sixth point, suicide, or "death by pilot," because it was too hard to believe.

You don't get to fly 777s in this industry by accident.

There are two indisputable facts:
1. Physics ensures the wings will work, and
2. To be paid to sit in the 777 flight deck requires years of dedication, study and training.

It's possible to get onto a 737 or an A320 as a trainee, but the 777 is the highest level of airliner.

Although three pilots before the crash of MH370 had carried out suicide, (post-Germanwings, now four), there are hundreds of thousands who have professionally plied their trade for entire careers over decades, and there are about 130,000 who are still doing so. So, for me, it was always impossible to think that the pilots of MH370 would do anything other than try to complete a safe flight.

Psych testing has come a long way since it was introduced by the US Army to find entry-level soldiers after World War 2. In the late 1960s, as personnel managers adopted it as a selection tool, a few business leaders complained that psych tests were designed to find cannon fodder. But who wanted cannon fodder? When a Carrier air-conditioning high-flyer secretly filled in his own company's selection psych test, he found that he didn't even qualify as a janitor for his own corporation.

When large airlines started using psych testing to sift through the hundreds of applicants for each job, pilots naturally became skeptical, branding human resources types as "head-shrinkers." That attitude still exists among old hands. Pilots are sensitive to anyone who can clip their wings.

In the intervening 50 years, the personnel department has been rebranded human resources and the tests have become scientific, none more so than those selecting airline pilots. Psychologists and even psychiatrists began appearing as department heads and their approval was needed for all new hires. One airline in Australia had three office floors dedicated to human resources, headed by a top psychologist who developed their own psych test targeting 12 factors designed to find pilots who had similar qualities to their most revered captains. Nowadays pilots take these tests seriously.

Not only do airlines have to qualify for insurance for each Boeing 777 (a USD $260 million asset before you start buying the addictive, expensive, spare parts), the cost of a crash may destroy the entire company. My experience with extensive psych testing has been limited to Australian and Middle Eastern airlines and so it came as a shock to read a BBC story that said European airlines, prior to Germanwings, were not psych testing candidates.[53]

The current test for most airlines is about 430 questions and is guaranteed to uncover any self-harm tendencies. One airline's psychiatrist was quizzed as to why there were about 10 suicide-type questions in the latest version of the test. She replied:

"We have found that if you ask a person five times, in different ways, if they are suicidal … they will tell you."

She went on to mention that the test is given to all their employees, and that a few people had " … put their hand up and we have been able to help them." Though she also stressed that none of the people who had shown suicidal tendencies had been pilots.

Airlines choose us for this job because, when all the psych-test results come in, we are consistent at "pattern-matching" and more than a little scared of dying. And that makes for a safety-conscious pilot. Daredevil pilots rarely get into airlines.

To anyone who has worked within the Asian culture, the chances of a younger pilot having the nerve to lock out his superior, and do a Germanwings, are not worth considering.

So we won't.

7. MULTIPLE FAILURES

A wise old skipper who had been a fast-jet instructor for the Royal Air Force wears different socks, never from the same pair, whenever he flies. Superstitious? Not at all.

An expert in risk management, he is a true believer in the modern airline industry where everything is based on "what are the chances of …?" He figures that the chances of a bomb going off on an airliner are millions to one. But the chances of a bomb going off in a plane whose captain has different socks are *billions* to one.

It's stupid, it makes no sense; but it's probably true. Either way, he is still working and not one bomb has gone off on any of his flights.

Under the rules known as Extended-range Twin-engine Operational Performance Standards (ETOPS),[54] (we call it "engines turning or passengers swimming"), the risk managers now allow the two-engined Boeing 787 to fly to a point that is five and a half hours from a suitable airport, have a cargo fire, depressurization or engine failure, and fly to safety. In the old days, you weren't allowed to go further than an hour from an airport.

When a British Airways 777 had a double-engine flameout and crashed at Heathrow,[55] it still didn't lower the airline's ability to do ETOPS flights. You have to have three events in a year within the ETOPS sector (the remote part of the flight) before your ETOPS approval is canceled. The remaining BA 777 fleet took off again the next morning even though the cause of the crash was a complete mystery.

The experts do risk analysis on everything and ask, "What are the chances of THAT happening?" With the chances so slim, *until they are wrong,* they are right.

The day after the industry loses a twin-engined jet over the Pacific Ocean due to a depressurization, engine failure or cargo fire, everything will change and they will be producing four-engined Boeing 747s and Airbus A380s ever after.

This new philosophy, produced by statisticians, is at odds with pilots' view of things, suspended 10 kilometers above the Indian Ocean at night, hours from an airport. And not even a good airport at that. During the monsoon. With a runway that's ever so short, and has no centerline lighting or grooving (which means it's slippery).

We often imagine how the statisticians would go, if one sat beside us when an engine failed:

"No worries, just operate these buttons and levers here and we should be OK to fly for 2 hours and 59 minutes to the nearest airport. Don't be nervous, our only other engine doesn't know this one has failed." (As you silently hope the engine failure was not caused by a contaminated batch of fuel.)

To go five and a half hours with a broken aircraft would take extreme courage. At Auckland,

I used to tip my hat to the pilots about to embark on the 11 hour 30 minute LAN800 Boeing 787 flight to Santiago, Chile, knowing they would be nudging the South Pole in a twin-engined aircraft.

The discussion about ETOPS has no relevance to MH370; its route was always within an hour of an airport.

With the chances of having a catastrophic problem being so remote, how much do you have to know these days?

When I was a shiny, brand new first officer you had to know everything. Seriously, back then every Boeing 727 pilot could draw you the electrical system, and even the inside of the engines. I have no idea why. The engine either worked or it didn't. And if you think they'd let a sprog FO tear down a Pratt & Whitney JT8D engine, you'd be mistaken. The cabin crew didn't even trust us with the coffee maker. (And there is not a pilot flying who understands the entertainment system. Thank God for pursers.)

By the time I moved to the Airbus in 1997, they had realized that, after giving us enough information about the engines to make us appear wise at parties, they'd only spend the time teaching us information that could be useful to us in a crisis.

Airbus information is:
- Must know
- Need-to-know
- Nice-to-know

… plus the obscure stuff the examiners ask to make you think they are clever. The only response to such questions is OIC ("Oh! I see…"). Never, ever, argue with examiners, or your fellow sim partner is going to miss the start of the game on television. Not cool.

These days, with every aircraft having 21 systems and about 135 computers, there is a limit to how much information you can retain. These are robots we are operating. Most of the game is simplifying a system to make it easy to remember and, more importantly, recalling where to turn to in the 777's 2,450-page flight crew operations manual. (The A380's manual is 8,214 pages and now only comes in eBook format.)

Which brings me to "multiple failures" and Occam's razor. William of Occam, who died in 1347 at the age of 50, was a scholar and theologian who came up with a problem-solving concept that is still used today. His concept, which cuts to the center of the issue, is therefore called a "razor."

Loosely translated, "the simplest explanation is usually the correct one."

When investigating plane crashes, don't try complicating matters; it normally takes only one thing to fail.

Airplanes are so reliable these days, and air traffic systems are so much safer, with alarms that ring if aircraft are in conflict. There have been many engineering advances, and there is now also double checking of every action performed, with both systems and operational procedures each "pressure tested" by external authorities and approved by the regulators. It's very safe.

Everything you see on *Air Crash Investigation* was fixed by 1990. The cause of *your* plane crash hasn't been discovered yet, so there's no need to watch.

Planes crash, usually, because of only one failure. Which is bad enough when you come to think of it.

The chances of multiple failures occurring are so remote that the manufacturers no longer train for them. (That is to say, yes, an engine failure leads to the hydraulics and electrical generator systems failing for that engine, but there is no need to train for an engine failure and, say, nose-wheel steering failure occurring together. They never do.)

The chances of having two unrelated events, and then a third are infinitesimal, and not even required for aircraft certification.

So, despite some plausible theorizing and excellent research, I have to discount Mick Gilbert's elaborate method of doing away with MH370.[56] You can find it on the web link and in newspapers whose editors don't mind frightening the horses. His theory is the ultimate "bad day."

Gilbert contends a windscreen fire brought down the aircraft. Not a normal windscreen-heat element, short-circuit fire, but something catastrophic which breaches the structural integrity, leading to failure of three layers of glass, gold heat-meshing, and laminating plastic.

Thankfully, windscreen fires are a fairly rare occurrence. But one does happen each year or so, and a 777 built around the same time as MH370 had an incident.

But Gilbert's theory assumes that not only the airframe had a faulty windscreen (possible) but there was also a leaking oxygen system.

For his theory to work, the plane had to suffer a windscreen failure. Masks on immediately. While exiting his seat to get the fire extinguisher the captain pulled off his oxygen hose causing a flash fire in the oxygen-rich air, which took him out. The air was supposedly oxygen rich because of a slow leak and now pure oxygen poured into the cockpit via the torn hose. (You could have put your finger over the hole and called for help on the PA if you weren't on fire).

Yes, it is possible, if you imagine that the cockpit air is *not* being changed every three minutes, being drawn down at floor level away from the supposed fire. Hopefully the oxygen-rich air he describes would never have reached window level.

After doing away with the captain, he then supposed that the most up-to-speed FO in the company (and maybe the world that night) had forgotten how to do an emergency descent. Even with his eyes shut.

Gilbert's theory also fails to deal with how the boundary layer works. Bugs get stuck on airplane windscreen wiper blades just like they do on cars, and they can remain there, without being blown off, from Los Angeles to Sydney. Would the air actually come inside a broken windscreen being used as the outflow valve, or would it form a pressure bubble? You wouldn't want to be the bunny who has to test it.

Although anything is possible, by the end of his multiple failure scenario I was screaming: "All too hard!"

But thanks, Mick, for realizing that the pilots were heroes.

In a world where every crash has Professor James Reason's "Swiss Cheese" model[57] lining up multiple errors and causes to produce one failure, the idea of multiple failures is too complicated when there is always a simple method, as we shall see.

8. LITHIUM BATTERY FIRE

Like the old magnesium wheels in cars, lithium battery fires are virtually inextinguishable until everything burnable is consumed, and they give off horrid smoke. After UPS Flight 6 crashed in Dubai on September 3, 2010, the world changed for aircrew. The crash report[58] details the issues with these batteries and is recommended reading if you wish to gain detailed knowledge on the matter.

MH370 was carrying lithium batteries as cargo. The shipment, from Motorola Solution Penang, contained 133 items in one IATA standard "unit load device" (ULD) weighing 1,990 kg, and a further 67 "loose" packages on an IATA standard pallet weighing 433 kg. "Loose" is a technical term; the items were extremely well-packaged.

Of the total consignment of 2,453 kg, only 221 kg were lithium-ion batteries, the rest were chargers and radio accessories.

They were packaged correctly and it is my opinion that they did not catch fire together like the UPS 747 crash in Dubai. If they had, the fire would have raged until the fuselage or systems were destroyed, and the plane would have crashed in Malaysian or Indonesian airspace within 30 minutes.

Investigators have forensically examined the shipment; you can see all the details of how they were packaged in the investigator's report entitled "MH370 Factual Information."[59]

The documentation released shows that they were not contained in equipment but were packed as batteries in accordance with IATA's Dangerous Goods Regulations (DGR) manual. The size and capacity of the batteries, however, did not qualify them as "dangerous goods" and they did not appear on the Notification To Captain (NOTOC) that the captain signed. We can assume that Captain Shah had no idea they were onboard.

Subsequent to the fallout after the UPS crash investigation, the carriage of lithium batteries has been changed. Now captains are advised of any carried as cargo, but this had not been introduced until after MH370.

A few types of batteries cannot be on passenger aircraft, and Fedex has decided to add further restrictions for its cargo-only flights. Pilots do a special course on this, and the fire-fighting procedures are practiced by cabin crew since most lithium batteries are carried by passengers in their laptops, tablets and phones.[60]

The placement within the cargo hold shows that the 1,990 kg ULD was positioned in 22R, on the right-hand side of the forward cargo compartment, aft of the door.

The 463 kg pallet with the 67 "loose" packages was loaded in the last position, 44R of compartment 4 on the right-hand side. Immediately rearward of this position is the bulk cargo compartment, where they put strollers, wheelchairs, surfboards and rush cargo. In this case, it only contained two strollers and 6 kg of cargo, probably the UPS satchels.

It's my contention that the quality control of the lithium battery shipments associated with the contract, the professionalism of the MAS systems and cargo operation, and the location of the batteries in the holds, using all the knowledge gained from the UPS crash, made it a safe operation. The cargo handling side of the industry was quick to act. There were 69 flights to Beijing carrying identical loads of the batteries between January and May 2014 from Motorola Solution Penang. If they had caught fire, the aircraft would not have flown long at all before suffering massive system damage with a raging, inextinguishable fire. While the smoke would be contained in the cargo compartment, or vented overboard if it breached the liners, the pilots would have had time to tell the world. The pilots of UPS 6, whose fire was on the main deck of the cargo 747, were still able to tell everyone.

With such a fire in the cargo hold, Captain Shah and FO Hamid may even have landed in Penang or Langkawi in time.

RECAPPING

- From Kazakhstan, to chasing and shadowing, some theories are too crazy.
- A bomb causes a wide debris field and this was discounted after parts were discovered in the Indian Ocean.
- Explosive decompression is exciting and one of our party tricks. Very

survivable.

- Accidental shoot-down is discounted due to the time of day and the fact that this was a regular daily flight. Also produces a large debris field.
- Mid-air collision is discounted because there was no traffic, and after parts were discovered in the Indian Ocean.
- Hijack is discounted because there is no claim of responsibility or evidence that anyone on board had motives.
- Hypoxia is discounted because the climb to 45,000 feet did not happen, plus it is not a reliable way to kill people quickly, and at the same rate, in a cabin full of oxygen masks and portable cylinders.
- Loss of control is discounted after the parts were discovered in the Indian Ocean.
- Suicide is ruled out since there is no proof of an issue in the pilots' background checks. Plus, a suicidal captain couldn't help to gain notoriety by crashing into the Petronas Towers.
- Multiple failures, while possible, are too difficult. The chances are too infinitesimal. Occam's razor says the simple answer is nearly always right; a

single failure with multiple systems degradation is more plausible.
- A fire in the shipment of lithium batteries would have elicited at least one radio call since they were in the cargo compartment.

From The Logbook:

How much do you have to know? #2
You can simplify things a bit too much though.
I flew with a pilot who declared the engine was a "BRT."
Even I knew that wasn't right: our airplane had the world's most popular jet engines, the CFM-56.
He admonished me, and announced that BRT stood for the "big round thing" under the wing.
He called the aircraft we were flying the "GBJ", which stood for "great big jet."
One morning at Sydney Airport, sitting at the holding point waiting to take off, he nodded towards the United 747 crossing over the piano keys only meters in front of us: "VGBJ."
I raised an eyebrow.
He answered knowingly:
"VERY great big jet."

MY ANALYSIS

Chris Goodfellow is an experienced Canadian instrument-rated multi-engine pilot. I believe he was closer to the mark than anyone when he theorized that a fire sent smoke into the cockpit and incapacitated the pilots. BBC's Anthony Zurcher should write him an apology after dismissing his claims with the headline "An MH370 theory that was simple, compelling *and wrong*."[61]

Nearly all uncontrollable aircraft fires have started within the first two hours of flight. And sometimes, a failed air-conditioning system will pump smoke straight into the cabin and cockpit.

As well as the lithium batteries, MH370 carried 4,566 kg of mangosteen fruit in four locations. All were in the rear cargo hold. Fresh fruit, and even cut flowers, can give off heat and fumes. Technically, ripening fruit continues to take in oxygen and emit gas in the form of carbon dioxide (unlike trees which do the opposite) and ethylene. Because of this, the industry even has special standards and handling procedures.

MAS had a competent track record of

shipping both the fruit and the batteries on the Beijing run, with 85 shipments of the fruit, and 36 flights carrying both fruit and batteries.

While both cut flowers and fruit have been known to set off smoke detectors in cargo compartments, resulting in deploying fire extinguishers and diversions, the more likely culprit is something in a passenger's baggage that has been smoldering since it was packed. A spare, fully charged laptop battery squeezed against a paperclip, hairpin or coin shorting the connectors is enough to do it. So could medical oxygen generators, camping stoves and other things listed on your ticket as 'dangerous goods' (that you could read about if you bothered).

Five tablet computers without packaging, being brought home as presents and squeezed into someone's luggage until one broke, may also be enough.

Cargo fires are fairly simple, if not nerve-wracking, for passenger airliner crews. You seal off the forward or rear cargo compartment at the press of a button then hit the fire extinguisher bottles. Within a minute there is no oxygen in the compartment (sad if you are carrying animals), and the second extinguisher is then dribbled-in over the next three hours (or five and a half hours for the Boeing 787) until you can land. Pilots have no desire to test the effectiveness of the system, preferring to land as soon as possible.

We call the cargo fire extinguisher button "the decision switch." In a second, you have made the decision to leave the other cargo compartment *without* fire protection, since both Boeing and Airbus believe it saves weight to only have one system and thus direct the protecting halon "agent" to the compartment in need. The regulators and their accountant friends have agreed that the chances of having fires in both compartments at the same time is not worth calculating. They probably never fly over large oceans, or the polar region, so they aren't worried. But for pilots, the matter is on our minds every time we are out of sight of land.

MH370 most likely didn't have a cargo fire because the pilots were not shouting on the radio, which is the next thing you do after you've pressed those two buttons.

So was it in the cabin?

The first thing about a fire in the cabin is that you don't have much time. A fully developed fire in an aircraft is a life-threatening situation. The record for staying alive and aloft is about 22 minutes; 19 is the average.

You land—at an airport, in the mountains, on the snow or the sea—or you die. Thankfully, our fully trained fire fighters, moonlighting as cabin crew, put out 99.99 percent of cabin fires. They are even trained to fight lithium battery fires. It's when we are ferrying empty planes without cabin crew, or fly freighters, that we become extra vigilant.

Other locations for fires are wheel wells, engines and wings. In the case of wheel wells, raising the gear with a seized brake and setting fire to hydraulic fluid is a possibility, and we have procedures for that. For engines, well, there is a fire inside each one all the time anyway and the systems to extinguish any fire that develops in the nacelle surrounding the engine are well developed. It looks spectacular from the passenger cabin (thankfully pilots can't see it), but engines can still deliver thrust even if the engine is on fire, and we usually don't put them out until we reach a safe height. Sadly, Air France's burning Concorde had the engine shutoff too close to the ground and never made it high enough to divert to nearby Le Bourget.

As for wings, if a wing burns through, the airplane will no longer be an airplane, simple. It will be a piano falling from 10 kilometers high. So the fix is a rapid descent and emergency landing. Modern systems are so safe, I can't think of an airborne wing fire that has occurred in the last 30 years[62].

Smoke events are much more regular. Air-conditioning systems fail and, in some cases, smoke is pumped into the cabin at an alarming rate. Aerotoxic,[63] a website tracking cases as they occur, reports that one smoke or fumes event happens every 2,000 flights. 1,300 fume events every day. Some aircraft types are repeat offenders—the BAE 146 has a checkered history—but the 777 is not overly representative.

In Australia, over 1,000 events were reported to authorities in a five-year period, prompting the ATSB and CASA to produce a special report.[64]

For aircrew in the cabin it is difficult trying to find the source, especially at night, if smoke pours in through vents all over the aircraft. Crew have been known to discharge extinguishers at vents at floor level in the belief that there was a fire below. Hence the need for calm communication with the flight deck.

The clue "It's coming from the vents!" will make it easy for pilots to apply the drill and turn off the left or right air-conditioning pack (system) with an immediate result. The problem is that the entire cabin is soon covered in smoke and it's hard to distinguish if the problem has ceased.

Questioning witnesses is tricky. It's easy to ask:

"Do you smell smoke?" rather than the correct "Do you smell anything?"

If I tell you to smell smoke in an airplane, you probably will.

Other sources of smoke, such as faulty galley equipment or a passenger seat, are easier to deal with as the area is localized.

The latest industry problem is the passenger dropping their smartphone down between the motorized seats in premium cabins. Telling them to not move the seat receives a similar response as a "wet paint" sign on a park bench. Soon the phone is crushed and we have a potential lithium battery fire.[65] (The video link from this endnote shows the amount of smoke from a crushed phone. Once seen, it's something you'll never forget.)

Either way, air-conditioning smoke, while arguably carcinogenic, doesn't kill in seconds and pilots have time to get their masks on if they experience a whiff. Turning off all air-conditioning, reconfiguring the valves to extract the smoke, performing a rapid descent, and depressurizing the aircraft to introduce fresh air directly from outside fixes the problem.

It's the uncontrollable fire that keeps us awake at night.

In 2010, lives, and procedures, changed forever when lithium batteries sparked a fire on the main deck of UPS Flight 6 shortly after takeoff from Dubai. A Boeing 747 freighter with two pilots on board, the flight was headed towards Europe, and, at the time of the fire, was in Bahrain ATC airspace. Instead of diving into the closest airport at Doha, the crew opted to return to Dubai, the airport they knew. In such a scenario, literally seconds count. Within two and half minutes of the alarm, and to save precious time turning back to Dubai, the captain disengaged the autopilot and hand-flew the aircraft. But ultimately time ran out.

The investigation's report makes chilling reading.[66]

The smoke on the flight deck had become so great that the crew not only couldn't see the instruments, but were also having trouble with their oxygen. After his mask system failed, the captain left his seat to go in search of supplemental oxygen. He never returned, and the first officer was then left to struggle alone in a pitch-black, smoke-covered cockpit. Zero visibility also meant he was unable to change radio frequency, and so had to stay with the one he had—Bahrain's sector controller. As UP6 headed out of range, Bahrain engaged several relay aircraft to communicate between the struggling plane and ATC. One of the relay pilots, on his last flight before retirement, was captaining the Dubai sheikh's 747. His final exchanges with the UPS first officer—a few minutes' radio conversation in the last half-hour of a long career—will no doubt haunt him to the grave.

After he told me his story, I was haunted too. And still am. I was working on the A380 at the time, and we were regularly carrying 545 souls. After this tragedy, a few of us developed a technique.

For at least the first two hours of every flight we have the approach charts of the nearest airport already displayed on our electronic charts. After obtaining the current weather via ACARS for the closest airports, we program the suitable runway into our flight management system's secondary flight plan. The secondary plan is then set up for the full approach and landing at each airport we pass. The A380 can store three secondary plans, allowing you to leapfrog the emergency airports as you go. For the emergency airports, we place 100 nm rings around them on the navigation display—ideal descent points—to aid our situational awareness.

> The procedures, in the event of a serious fire, sees the captain take control to:

1) Descend the aircraft to the altitude of the start of the instrument approach or the minimum safe altitude, terrain permitting. Turn the altitude knob and pull "Open Descent."
2) Activate the secondary flight plan, with a couple of keystrokes.
3) Select "Direct To" the start of the instrument landing approach and activate.
4) Select "MAX autobrake" so the plane will stop on the runway, regardless of who is still alive.
5) Arm the instrument landing system.

After seven seconds of button-flicking the plane is now going to fly down to the start of the approach, intercept it, land and stop. (The A380 has 22 wheels; 16 with brakes. It stops in a hurry if you ask it to.) All you have to do is apply speed brake to increase the rate of descent and decide on the speed.

Flaps and gear depends on your location and time available. Your mission is to be the fastest pilot in the world to 20 miles before slowing up.

Meanwhile, you're calling "Mayday" to clear the airspace, get help from ATC, and alert the rescue fire fighting services (RFFS) on the ground. Even if you can't see due to smoke, ATC can give you your altitudes and speeds. The Airbus altitude knob has a nifty feature; each click is worth 1,000 feet and by selecting speed you can bleed the speed back in time to get flaps and gear out.

As the initial approach point nears you can select gear down and the aircraft will wait until you are at a safe speed before lowering the wheels. When the wheels drop out you will have a clue as to the speed and you can then start configuring the first stage of flap.

Working with ATC, and provided the approach arming system engages, there is no reason why the plane couldn't do an auto-land and stop on the runway. Within 90 seconds, all the passengers will be disembarked, even if half the exits are unusable.

The first officer runs the "Smoke, Fire or Fumes" checklist, configuring fans and valves to dump the smoke overboard and then turning off electrical or air-conditioning systems, one at a time, to isolate the problem.

When smoke gets too thick, the FO switches

to the "Smoke Removal" checklist, which gives up trying to troubleshoot the source. The new goal is to depressurize the cabin to obtain fresh air and put the aircraft into emergency electrical configuration. All major electrical and air-conditioning sources are now dead so the source of the smoke *should* be gone. The captain has to hand-fly from hereon, as there is not enough electricity to run the FO's side of the ship, or the autopilots—another reason why pilots may delay switching checklists.

Until the ram air turbine (RAT) drops out (a fancy word for a Cessna-sized propeller) and starts spinning to provide a tiny amount of electrical and hydraulic power, you are on batteries that will last about 20 minutes. After a pause, a few gut-wrenching generator clunks and screen flickers, the RAT's generator starts and you have enough electricity to get home. Much more than when she was on the batteries, but only enough power to run a bus. In normal service, each engine generator could power an entire village.

Doing this for real is the day you earn all your retirement benefits. We do it in the simulator during conversion training and at least once every three years on a rotating systems cycle. Hamid would have done it less than two months before the MH370 flight. Captain Shah was most likely so used to running it in the simulator when testing candidates that he could've done the procedure blindfolded.

After the crash of UPS 6, most airlines have added it to handling sim sessions as a confidence-builder. Handling sims are usually conducted every six months in between the licensing simulator exams. They are training only, designed to give pilots practice in hand flying.

Few of us imagined this scenario for MH370, because there was no radio contact. The first thing pilots do in real emergencies is share the problem with as wide an audience possible. "Mayday Mayday Mayday" gets everyone's attention. I have heard it twice in my career and it chills the blood. Everyone in earshot grabs a pen and starts writing what they hear.

In MH370's case, there was nothing.

But there was that "turn-back," as the Malaysian Air Force called it, from waypoint Igari on the border with Vietnam, and at the end of that turn were Penang and Langkawi Airports.

Langkawi island receives a high amount of tourist traffic. It's also where Hamid learnt to fly, met his fiancé, and is the stomping ground of every Malaysian 737 pilot. Both men would have known every frequency, approach, runway, altitude restriction … every hill. And remember, Penang was Captain Shah's birthplace.

If a fire had started in the upper rear right-hand rack in the main equipment center (also known as the "avionics compartment" or "E and E bay") underneath the forward cabin and flight deck, then maybe the ACARS and radios were gone before anything became apparent. The pilots were making all the appropriate calls and dialed the correct emergency transponder frequency, unaware that nothing was getting out to the aerials.

When you make your Mayday call you end it with "…standby!" because you don't want to be assailed by the controller who, you imagine, has opened a huge book full of questions and starts behaving like you had just pressed his start button:

"MH370, Mayday acknowledged, go ahead number of souls on board…"

Your brain overloads. What the? The same number we had for take off … I don't know, ask the company! I am not going to stop doing this procedure to go and look up the load sheet for the number of passengers and crew.

So it's easy to finish every emergency call with "… standby!", and get back to them afterwards.

The rules of airline flying are encapsulated in the axiom Aviate, Navigate, Communicate: Let's get this thing under control, point it somewhere safe and talk later.

It's possible that after setting the emergency transponder code, doing a mayday call and being distracted by the action, they didn't realize they had not heard a response.

Due to the location of the compartment,

although the sealing of the hatch is smoke-proof, the smoke may have seeped into the forward cabin as well as the cockpit. You could expect smoke warnings from the forward cargo compartment, the main equipment center and even the toilets.

A possible event that springs to mind is an inextinguishable fire, maybe lithium batteries or a large portable oxygen generator in passenger baggage stacked up high in the right-hand forward position of compartment one; something that would cause a small but intense fire against the cargo liner for longer than five minutes and hotter than 927 C, the design specification of the fabric. That's what would be needed to breach the liner, as specific tests on Boeing's cargo liners have shown.[67] On the other side of that compartment liner are the wiring looms associated with the back of an important rack within the main equipment center. The smoke from that loom may produce enough poisonous smoke to kill. While the differential pressures are designed to protect the crew from smoke, what systems could have been taken out? (Although the differential pressures failed to protect the pilots on UPS6.)

The number of alarms going off from smoke is enough to numb the mind, let alone the alarms from systems affected by the wiring loom being breached.

Let's imagine that they didn't pre-plan a secondary flight plan. Most crews don't.

The warnings may have started simultaneously: "fire cargo fwd"; "smoke lavatory"; "smoke equipment cooling."

Captain Shah would have called:

"Smoke, Fire and Fumes—I have control!"

As an instinctive reaction, his right hand may have moved in an arc that started the stop watch, turned on the aircraft landing lights, and seat-belt sign. That's what I was taught to do by a clever Zimbabwean captain:

- Start timing because time has a habit of moving slower than you think
- Be seen by other aircraft
- Secure the cabin
- Get ready for action.

A three-second hand wave culminating in asking your first officer:

"What do you think happened?"

This is good crew resource management that sometimes elicits an opposite viewpoint to your own thoughts; we are not as smart as we think we are.

As the emergency is annunciated the captain assumes the role of handling pilot and the first officer becomes monitoring pilot. Shah took over and started the turn left to Penang. This is what appeared on the primary radar paints as an abrupt turn to the left, a constant turn onto a southwesterly heading.

A 777 in cruise would chew up at least 20

track miles (37 km) doing a normal, shallow turn so as not to spill the coffee. Captain Shah may have figured that the fastest way to do a u-turn, get down and across the peninsula was to disconnect the autopilot and hand-fly, achieving a faster turn rate than the autopilot. Save time. Good decision. It's what the UPS 6 captain did, and what captains do in the simulators.

He probably disconnected the autopilot and turned left, rolling into a 30-degree turn. Maybe 45 degrees. If the radar paints are accurate they can calculate the bank angle he used.

With smoke you have to put your masks on and use 100 percent oxygen, but Captain Shah may have wanted to do the turn first and Hamid may have wanted to knock off the first few items of the checklist before donning their masks. It's understandable. The actual checklist says:

"Don oxygen masks and smoke goggles, **if needed**."[68] *[My emphasis.]*

Firstly, in most sims the theatrical smoke used, like at rock concerts, isn't deadly. Secondly, your nose is the greatest asset in determining if the source of the smoke is electrical or air-conditoning, and third, as soon as your mask goes on your world reduces to what is in front of you. It's claustrophobic. You feel like you are single pilot on the only day you need someone else's help. It's worse if you wear reading glasses.

Unlike depressurization drills where the

mask goes on immediately, no questions asked, with smoke and fumes, if there are none in the cockpit, there is a tendency not to use the masks, yet. That's where the BBC article, which belittles Chris Goodfellow, is wrong.

If the smoke is in the cargo compartment, lavatories or the back cabin, the masks are rarely used immediately, if at all.

Smoke, Fire and Fumes is normally a communications exercise with the cabin crew if they are fighting a cabin fire. The captain sits there on the intercom talking to the cabin crew member designated as The Communicator, building up a picture from what they are seeing, while the first officer flies. It is much easier to conduct the initial troubleshooting with masks off, so your fellow pilot is in the loop.

For other types of fires the captain takes control of the aircraft and radios while the FO does their checklist, leaving their masks off until they smell smoke. It's much faster and you can achieve a great deal in a short amount of time.

But on rare occasions that'd be the wrong thing to do.

Ever since the 1985 Airtours 737 fire in Manchester, all airliner seats, curtains, floor and wall coverings have been fire-blocked to prevent ignition. We have developed a false sense of security.

Plastic sources of fire can go up like they do

at home. Burning or melted plastics means poisonous, dense, black smoke in the form of deadly carbon monoxide and hydrogen cyanide gas. Depending on the concentration of the smoke, it's possible that as few as two or three breaths can cause loss of consciousness, even death.

For all we know, which is nothing, the fire may have been a mobile phone in a pilot's nav-bag setting fire to a plastic folder jammed full of sheets of paper in plastic sleeves. Or Mick Gilbert's windscreen. But I am leaning to something more insidious; otherwise their masks would have been on first.

The Organization for the Prohibition of Chemical Weapons (OPCW) lists hydrogen cyanide's symptoms:

> "If hydrogen cyanide has been inhaled, the initial symptoms are restlessness and increased respiratory rate. Other early symptoms are giddiness, headache, palpitations and respiratory difficulty. These are later followed by vomiting, convulsions, respiratory failure and unconsciousness. If the poisoning occurs rapidly, e.g., as a result of extremely high concentrations in the air, there is no time for symptoms to develop and exposed persons may then suddenly collapse and die."[69]

It is possible that there was a delay trying to

communicate with the cabin crew, who were already dealing with black smoke seeping from the main equipment center's access hatch below the purser's station; the hatch cover has a seal, but it may have been ineffective.

As the aircraft settled onto the south-westerly heading, Captain Shah may have been incapable of putting on his mask or initiating descent.

Maybe FO Hamid's actions, before he too succumbed, achieved the goal. Perhaps the first actions on the checklist stopped the electrical short, which stopped the melting plastic of the unit in question, or maybe the extinguishing agent from the cargo compartment seeped through and put out the now-dead loom after the source of the fire had run out of propellant. Or maybe the plastic on the wiring loom took hold.

Maybe, like UPS 6, the crew oxygen system was damaged or destroyed by fire. The oxygen bottle is on the left hand side of the main equipment center. There is one smoke hood on the flight deck but they are difficult enough to get on in the classroom every year during emergency revalidation, let alone in a smoke-filled flight deck, at night, when you realize your oxygen supply has just been cut. We will never know.

What we do know is that although things were not working, somehow the aircraft and in-flight entertainment system's maintenance function continued to do its job. Twice it initiated and five times it answered the satellite's handshakes. The main satellite components were above door number three, away from the main equipment centre, although circuit breakers for the system were in there.

If the cabin crew had not heard from the pilots after repeated calls they would have applied the approved security technique and opened the flight deck door. The smoke which disabled the pilots would have flooded into the cabin.

The Station Night Club on Rhode Island, which caught fire in 2003, killing 100 people,[70] was fully enveloped in less then six minutes. The main cause of death was carbon monoxide and hydrogen cyanide gas, given off after fireworks set fire to polyurethane sound deadening.

There have been 37 nightclub fires since the first in 1929. Since the Station Night Club disaster there have been 11 more fires with a toll of 846 deaths and over 2,000 injuries. Hidden behind facades and laneway entrances, we don't seem to learn. Charged with alcohol or drugs, attending a night club can be a dangerous way to end your evening.

It wasn't until cameras were trained on London's Grenfell Tower fire in June 2017 that the public saw, in real time, the effects of flash fire and toxic smoke.

In MH370's case, it was a more confined

area than a nightclub or residential tower; most of the passengers would have been asleep and simply never woke up. We hope.

Less than 10 minutes after it started, after its crew and passengers succumbed to smoke, the aircraft was now flying, autopilot off, all by itself. It happened so quickly that Captain Shah had not initiated the descent.

Something stopped the plane burning, if it ever was.

Perhaps Hamid, following the correct procedures for smoke, fire and fumes, turned off the passenger seats in-flight entertainment system and re-configured the recirculation and gasper fans to stop spreading the smoke around. These actions ensured that the killer smoke was eventually dumped overboard and despite the fact that everyone was dead, after a few hours maybe all looked relatively normal. Or perhaps the halon extinguisher finally won the battle with the passenger baggage; the lithium or propellant having been consumed, it was now a normal fire, eventually starved of oxygen.

Airliners are dynamically stable, that's why they have dihedral wings.[71] Which is why, when you look out the window, the wing's tip is higher than where it joins the fuselage. If you give the plane a small upset from turbulence, after oscillating a bit, it will return to normal flight. Fighter jets have the opposite: anhedral wings, which droop down the further out they are from the fuselage, making them unstable and easier to throw around the sky.

Airline pilots don't want to spill the coffee. Fighter pilots don't get any coffee; they have to work too hard.

With autopilot off, provided it doesn't fly into an active thunderstorm cell or the ground, the 777 should happily fly straight and level. Any turbulence oscillations eventually get smaller and smaller, then smooth out.

I know of one crew who had an autopilot failure during departure at Heathrow. After discussing with the company engineers and ATC that they were no longer "reduced vertical separation minima" (RVSM) compliant, the controllers provided them with headings and a 4,000 feet altitude buffer, allowing them to fly all the way to the Middle East. The captain, an ex South African Air Force high-speed jet instructor, said that they could fly hands-off for hours, the weight and inertia keeping the plane on course. The plane never moved from the assigned altitude.

Maybe, with autopilot off, MH370's left wing brushed a developing cumulous cloud after crossing the Malay Peninsula, and that was enough to turn it onto the west-nor-westerly heading.

Interacting with the clouds all the way up the Straits Of Malacca may account for the altitude variations. Although it must be noted that, as far as can be observed from primary radar paints, despite the conspiracy theories, it never descended below 31,000 feet.

The Intertropical Convergence Zone (ITCZ) is where the northern and southern hemisphere's trade winds collide. It is south of the equator in January and north in July. At the time of the crash, approaching equinox, it lay in the northern end of the Straits Of Malacca. An area of instability punctuated by both cumulous and cumulonimbus (Cb) clouds (thunderstorms), the zone makes for hard work for pilots as they weave around the bumpy weather. You usually can't fly straight for long.

There were no significant clouds forecast when MH370 flew towards Vietnam or back up the Straits Of Malacca. No Cb clouds forecast, and no lightning was recorded. An infrared satellite image taken 10 minutes after MH370 vanished shows the active cells that night were along the southern side of Java and east of Borneo.

Isolated cumulous clouds bubbling up to provide turbulence and change the aircraft's track may have been around, but the ITCZ was not its usual headache.

Something caused the first satellite handshake to occur before the major southerly turn. The login was from the aircraft to the ground station, maybe after a power interruption. Whether it was from external forces or a systems issue, we can only speculate. We do know, however, that the flight number and departure/destination tags appended to the satellite login in KLIA were gone. The satellite system was no longer connected to the flight management system; it was just a bare airplane logging in.

Minutes later, the start and finish positions during the unanswered call from MAS ops prove it was headed south. With autopilot off, maybe cloud activity caused the change in direction. After that position, on a line between Banda Aceh and Phuket, the southbound heading would have surely taken MH370 close by or into thunderstorms. It's a big sky, but there are always thunderstorms north and south of the equator and it's rare to fly so far without having to divert your track around them.

The average thunderstorm (Cb cloud) takes 20 minutes to build, is active for 20 minutes, then takes a further 20 minutes to dissipate into high-level cirrus clouds and low-level stratus. Just as it becomes active is when the lightning starts to occur. The time period between lightning flashes varies, but you can start with 90-second gaps if you are after a good photo. A Cb "cell" displayed on the weather radar shows up as a distinctive red blob, often breeding "daughter Cbs" and giving the impression of a single Cb that goes on for hours.

It is said that the energy released from a large Cb is equivalent to between 10 to 100 times the energy released by the nuclear bombs dropped on Japan to end the Second World War. If you could capture the energy released by "Huey," Darwin's daily thunderstorm during the wet season (and, ironically, its twin at Hue in Vietnam), then we wouldn't be in need of coal-fired power stations anymore.

About 80 percent of lightning stays inside the cloud, and with 100 strikes hitting planet earth per second (eight million a day and which keeps the ozone layer charged) one can only marvel at the number of strikes occurring within clouds. What appears to be one cloud flashes lightning for hours. It's not uncommon to take a photograph of a large Cb that puts the blue back into a pitch-black sky. Yet, during daylight, you rarely see the internal lightning, such is the brightness of our favorite star.

It is against company regulations in most airlines to venture closer than 20 nm to a Cb cloud during cruise flight. Air France 447 ran into two ITCZ Cbs and look what happened.

An old saying of mine is: "You fly into an active thunderstorm, you die." No wonder dogs don't like them.

The Faraday cage effect of the airliner's fuselage protects its occupants, but generators have been known to trip offline after a lightning strike.

If MH370 ran into a Cb without autopilot it is amazing that it was still flying, and is a testament to the 777's designers. Whatever headings it flew after emerging from such encounters is irrelevant. We don't need to know it's exact track. The refined 7th-arc radius from the satellite is where it was when it finally descended. By intersecting the arc with Dr. Griffin's latest drift analysis, we have a good starting point.

Only real flight tests in the warm moist air near the equator will prove if, given a slight climb from a cloud bubbling up beneath, a 777 with no autopilot will climb all the way and nestle itself into its service ceiling given its current weight and thrust settings. Eventually, MH370 probably settled into a cruise altitude, which extended its range; the investigators are betting it's 35,000 feet.

Finally, after five more handshakes with the satellite ground station and another unanswered phone call, the right engine ran out of fuel (because historically it was using more fuel than the left) and the scenario is as the investigators calculated. That is provided that the 777's Thrust Asymmetry Compensation (TAC) read the reducing engine parameters and introduced enough flight control compensation to keep the plane flying straight until the left engine flamed-out. Surely, then, it would have started slowing and maybe already started a shallow descent towards the single engine service ceiling of about 29,000 feet.

The ingenious TAC system is not dependant on the autopilot being connected, it just has to be turned on or not broken. The pre-flight checklist ensured that it was not turned off and MH370's Technical Log had no entry saying it was disabled. So we must assume it was on.

About 15 minutes after the first engine flameout, the left engine ran out of fuel. This may have produced startling results as the TAC had been using the flight controls to keep flying straight. Would the TAC provide a gentle release of the controls, or would it have been violent, as the rudder and ailerons lost their hydraulic power? Boeing can tell us what to expect. Either way, the power to the main electrical buses would have failed as the left engine generator died with its engine, causing the RAT to deploy and APU start automatically regardless of its switch position.

With 30 pounds of fuel within its pipe, it was enough to start the APU generator and start the satellite login process as the powerless airliner started down. Boeing's simulator work reckons the debris will be within 15 nm of the last flameout.[72]

On the other hand, if the engine parameters were not available, the TAC system damaged or turned off, the 777 would have gone straight in after the first engine flamed out, without the TAC to counter the drag of the failed engine. The left engine would have been delivering cruise power and she may have entered the water nose first, maybe at nearly twice the speed as the Space Shuttle Challenger.

Eagle-eyed engineers can spot the flaw: "Ah yes, but the aircraft made the 7th-arc login, so it must have been after the APU started its generator; and that would only happen after the second engine flamed out."

Not necessarily. Something caused the aircraft to make the first login as it made its way up the Straits Of Malacca, before it turned south. If that was a power interruption from a failure of the left engine generator, the 777 was flying on the right one all the while it headed south. Failure of the right engine then took out its only remaining generator, starting the APU and its generator, and initiating the login. By then she was going down, but with the left engine running. So we may be back to the 40 nm radius from the right engine flameout.

Regardless, much more time will be required in Boeing's high-tech engineering simulator since, as far as I can determine, all work to date has been predicated with at least one of the auto-pilot modes being engaged.

If MH370 went in like Swissair 111, on an angle, it may have disintegrated. But if it pointed straight down it may have plunged so far down into the ocean, compressing into "debris with wires sticking out," that the pressure took over and took her straight to the bottom like a broken ship or submarine, leaving only a relatively small area of frangible, lightweight, items to float west.

RECAPPING

- Lethal smoke, source unknown.
- Captain disconnected the autopilot and tried to turn towards Penang and the first officer tried to complete the initial Smoke, Fire or Fumes actions before putting on their masks.
- Both succumbed to smoke before getting the masks on.
- The aircraft continued without the autopilot, and at the mercy of the elements, the stability built in by the designers kept it flying.
- If it encountered severe weather its heading may have been affected.
- With TAC operating, even with no autopilot, the end-of-flight scenario assumes a 15 nm radius from the double-engine flameout entering the water, the intersection of the 7th arc at 35 degrees south.
- With no TAC and no autopilot operating, the end-of-flight scenario may assume the left engine operating at cruise power, possibly a higher rate of descent and a crash site within a 40 nm radius from the first flameout entering the water, the intersection of the 7th arc at 35 degrees south.

CONCLUSIONS

My theory is that the pilots of MH370 performed as any other Boeing 777 crew would in similar circumstances.

An event happened which caused the ACARS, transponder and radios to fail—either at the units, the wiring looms or between the units and aerials.

Captain Shah probably disconnected the autopilot in an effort to tighten his turn radius as he turned towards Penang in expectation of performing an emergency landing.

Both pilots were overwhelmed by poisonous smoke before they could get their masks on or commence a descent.

MH370 flew on, without autopilot, its progress affected by flying in and out of clouds.

Between the first "handshake" and the first sat-phone call to the aircraft, it entered an isolated cumulous cloud, or clouds, and emerged heading south.

The maintenance of altitude and steadiness of headings are a testament to the dynamic stability of the 777 and inertia associated with wide-bodied aircraft.

RECAPPING

- The pilots performed as well as any other crew.
- An emergency event developed, disabling ACARS, transponder and radios.
- Recognizing the urgency, Captain Shah disconnected the autopilot to decrease his turn radius to fly to Penang.
- Both pilots were overwhelmed by lethal smoke.
- The aircraft's progress was affected by the weather.
- The inherent stability of the 777, and its inertia, caused MH370 to fly for so long by itself.
- Simulator modelling will be required to determine how the MH370 would have performed with the autopilot off.
- The main debris is most likely located in the area suggested by Dr. David Griffin, within a radius of 40 nm at the intersection of the 7th arc and 35 degrees south. His position has been strengthened by the use of an actual Boeing 777 flaperon in tests in the seas off Hobart, and also by drift modelling done by the University Of Western Australia.

RECOMMENDATIONS

This book makes 13 urgent recommendations to the aviation industry.

1. Checklists

There is an issue with both the Boeing and Airbus "Smoke, Fire Or Fumes" checklists. At some stage, if the smoke gets too great, they recommend stopping this checklist and going for the "Smoke Removal" checklist.

It makes sense. But we don't have enough of these instances to know the psychology of humans doing these drills for real.

I have discounted FO Hamid having to make this switch of checklists. Since there was no descent initiation, I figure that the smoke disabled them too quickly.

Pilots are pattern-matching, completion nerds. They are manic about finishing the process or checklist. After every flight, the finishing of the process means a happy, safe airplane parked at the aerobridge. In many airlines, a final checklist will tell you to turn your phone back on, presumably so the company can call to thank you for making up time and saving fuel.

In the real world, does the first officer running the drill want to try "one more button," which may put the fire out, before switching to the Smoke Removal checklist? After all, changing checklists ensures they will *never* discover what caused the problem.

Maybe. This needs investigation. We need to know what pilots do in this actual situation.

Thankfully, the sample size is too small. But if the FO doing the checklist is young, having started as a cadet with the airline, how are we expecting him to know just when the smoke is becoming too great? Pilots with 20 years experience could spend hours in the classroom arguing over the right time to switch checklists without coming to an agreement. It's too difficult.

I believe that having conferences to fix a broken system is futile and recommend that pilots launch straight into a modernized Smoke Removal checklist *first* and then *later* re-introduce electrical and bleed-air systems after they have been tested as safe, after troubleshooting the culprit.

The Swissair 111 Final Report states:
> "The longer it takes to complete a prescribed checklist that is designed to de-energize a smoke source, the greater

the chance that the smoke source could intensify or become an ignition source and start a fire."[73]

As we have seen, turning off the air-conditioning in cruise should only result in the cabin climbing about 4,000 feet in the time it takes to discover which side, if any, is pumping smoke into the cabin. A by-product from the trouble shooting is that raising the cabin altitude will mean we can achieve depressurization faster if we need to perform a rapid descent (the difference between our altitude and that of the cabin will be closer).

2. Cameras

The 777 is now approaching 22 years old. It's time to develop better, modern, test equipment with high-definition cameras all over the plane, right throughout the cabin, like the A380, and in the cargo compartments, main equipment center and wheel wells.

Cameras should be focused along the walls of cargo holds, and we should be able to turn on lights and have a look.

For cold weather operations, we need floodlights and a high definition camera focused onto "representative surface," so we can make an informed decision after the holdover time has expired to see if the wings are contaminated. Looking out a passenger window to determine wing contamination, in a snowstorm, when the airplane is parked at the start of the runway, a kilometer from adequate lighting, is bordering on insanity.

Pilots should be able to look at the landing gear on the ground.

3. Test Equipment

We need a cockpit indicator, a glass tube showing a sample of each side's air-conditioning output, with a smoke sensor in it, so we can immediately identify which air-conditioning pack is producing smoke. In 50 years they will look back in disbelief, wondering how we could pump air into a cabin, completely changing it every three minutes, yet with no idea of the composition of that air.

4. Auto-Fire Suppression

These aircraft are robots. With approximately 135 computers, they move fuel around without our knowing, balance tanks and shift the centre of gravity so the plane flies most economically, and lots more. Maybe it's time for the cargo compartments to get robotic as well. They should have auto-fire suppression. Why rely on us to do what a computer can do in a second. Airborne? Smoke? What chemicals are in the smoke? Make a professional assessment, whammo! Fire out. Do it and let me know what you have done, please.

5. Fire Protection For BOTH Cargo Areas

While we are in charge, let's double the fire suppressant. One set of bottles for the forward compartment and one for the rear. And a special place to put dogs and cats where they are protected. The concept of a decision switch, (deciding to leave a compartment unprotected from fire), when you are flying over the north pole four hours from a safe haven, is not clever. Especially when the runway at that safe haven is only 2,500 meters long, covered in ice and snow, and the temperature, where you expect to disembark passengers in their summer clothing, is -35 C.

6. Find My Engine

See those engines out on the wing? Let's have a $20 app added to every monitored engine, which sends its latitude and longitude along with all the information the engineers want to know. Twenty-four million dollars for an engine and it doesn't have "find my phone." Seriously? With such an app, when a plane stops working, you can send the ships straight to the spot.

7. Ejectable Flight Recorders

Australian David Warren gave the world the black box flight recorder, so in his memory, lets modify his invention for the new age. Over time, as a result of crashes, there have been mandated improvements. The voice recorder requirement has been increased from the final 30 minutes to the final two hours. Battery life of the pinger has been extended, as a result of Air France 447 and MH370, from 30 days to 90 days. About time.

No-one took notice of the recommendation made in 1991 by the South African Board of inquiry into the loss of Boeing 747-244B (ZS-SAS), which stated:

> "It is recommended that:
>
> - The 'pinger' systems should be provided of two or more locators, one being operative for the first 30 days after impact, the other only taking over thereafter, to provide a total of 60 days of signals."[74]

Despite the US Navy having "ejectable recorders" since 1993, which are ejected from the aircraft just prior to impact, and the NTSB having recommended that they be introduced in new airliners since 1999 (at the meagre cost of $60,000 each), US Congress has blocked the bill three times. Post-MH370, Congressman David Price has been trying once again to launch the legislation.[75] Good luck to him. It appears that friends of the politicians don't want to spend that much.

8. Clever Pingers

MH370 has exposed issues with ping propagation in deep water. I recommend that all flight recorders be fitted with pressure sensors. When deeply submerged, they go into hibernation mode for seven to fourteen days to save their energy while the searchers get into position. In future, with better aircraft tracking, it can be expected that the general search area will be known immediately. When the players are assembled and there are people to listen, the recorder comes out of hibernation and starts pinging, but at double the power.

The benefit is that, as they are assembled, searchers can audio-map the area before the pinging starts, and nullify the background noise when the pinging begins.

This recommendation allows numerous submarines or deep water drones to be deployed to aid in providing multiple position lines. The voice and flight recorder pings themselves can be coded to aircraft tail numbers using short-burst Morse code to differentiate themselves from other noises and each other. (Swissair 111's voice and flight recorder pinger frequencies were the same, which confused the submarine trying to locate them).

9. Find My Aircraft

As a result of MH370, ICAO has decreed that by November 2018 all airliners must be capable of real-time tracking every 15 minutes. By 2021, an aircraft suffering an emergency will have to transmit its position every minute, reducing the search radius to within 6 nm.[76]

Some regulators require, and many airlines are already achieving, the 15-minute position fix. Every aircraft between Australia, New Zealand and the USA is achieving 14 minutes using the new Automatic Dependent Surveillance-Contract (ADS-C), which also increases to five-minute sampling during an abnormal event. The ATC can increase that further, from the controller's end, to almost real time.[77]

ADS-Contract[78] is different from ADS-B (Broadcast), which just tells the world where the aircraft is, allowing controllers and nearby aircraft to display its position. ADS-C means that there are two parties to the transaction: the airplane and the controller. After login, the ATC can interrogate the aircraft to determine chosen parameters, on a periodic, on-demand or event-driven basis; totally transparent to the pilots.

There are independent systems, such as

Canadian Skytrac,[79] which has been used in the oil and corporate flight industries for years. Using low-earth orbit satellites instead of ADS-B or C, such systems provide full world coverage and have already shown how successful they can be; in a recent helicopter incident, they transmitted parameter exceedance messages until the crash, allowing rescuers to go straight to the site.

New Zealand's Spidertracks,[80] another company using satellites, does much the same, and sends an SOS if the target aircraft loses power.

But what happens when the airplane's systems fail, like they probably did on MH370? The D in ADS stands for Dependant, meaning that it is dependant on the aircraft's navigation system.

If my recommendations are carried out, the first thing pilots will do in a smoke event is turn most things off, reinstating them only when they are known to be safe. Existing systems would have helped MH370 raise immediate attention over the Gulf of Thailand that something was wrong, but maybe not have tracked it to the crash site. We need more.

Lorne Cole is a Melbourne-based pilot with extensive airline and corporate experience. As Chief Executive Officer of JetCity[81] he oversees the operations of a fleet of six corporate jets, based at Essendon Airport, which conduct VIP and long-distance overwater air-ambulance operations around Asia, the South Pacific, Australia and New

Zealand. Cole explains:

"In time-critical flight operations, an 'estimated position' is not acceptable. I need to know exactly where my aircraft is."

After five years' development, Cole has launched Esstrack,[82] a product and service that takes David Warren's flight recorder to the new age. Fitting, since Melbourne's Essendon Airport was Warren's home base, and the airport to which his father was flying when he was killed in a plane crash in 1934. It was the loss of that aircraft over Bass Strait that prompted Warren to develop the flight recorder 19 years later.

Important systems shutting down do not bother Esstrack's A-TACS™ (Aviation Telecommunications & Communications System). Fully autonomous, with a tamper-proof power supply, it keeps on beaming encrypted data to its secure site in Switzerland. Cole's fleet is now using the comparatively low-cost device, which also works with ships, trucks and even caravans. (Apparently the stolen caravan market is quite lucrative in a country the size of Australia.) As well as a real-time flight recorder and position fixer, the system can also provide telecommunication and internet.

It's my recommendation that all passenger airliners immediately adopt Skytrac, Spidertracks, Esstrack or equivalent.

10. Oxygen Masks

Pilot oxygen masks don't work well with smoke.

As recently as the UPS 6 crash, pilots were using a mask that only covered the nose and mouth. Smoke goggles are fitted after the mask, then two little tubes are poked from the bottom of the goggles into the mask. Having managed that task, which is daunting in the classroom and probably near impossible on a smoke-filled flight deck at night, you then use the purge button on the mask to provide a burst of oxygen which flows up the tubes into the goggles, chilling your eyeballs and eradicating smoke. A newer version is less tricky, but not easy.

In the mid-90s, the new EROS mask provided quick access, all-in-one protection[83] and, yes, it was a stellar improvement. So we never complained.

But they have not been redesigned for 25 years. Pilots dread wearing them, especially with glasses. Let's find out what we are expected to do in the worst-case scenario and devise a mask to suit. It's time to improve the system.

11. Lithium Batteries

One of our small team of reviewers said: "Those lithium batteries ... they're off. We shouldn't carry them anymore."

If a belligerent passenger tried to board the aircraft with a lighter and a huge roll of magnesium ribbon the entire industry would applaud a captain for refusing to take him.

Personally, I trust the cargo industry and am only scared about lithium batteries brought on my aircraft by passengers. If it turns out that MH370 crashed because of a passenger's actions, I would have to agree with the reviewer. Passengers buy a ticket to fly, not die, and lithium batteries carried illegally in cargo baggage are scary. Really scary.

The Trump ban on carrying laptops and other lithium-powered devices in the cabin, relegating them to the cargo hold, flies in the face of ICAO and IATA guidelines. Really, if you are admitting that ISIS can produce an undiscoverable bomb in a laptop then we have bigger issues than where the laptop is positioned.

These recommendations are a radical departure from the way we do it now. But the way we do it now doesn't seem to be working.

12. Carry-On Baggage

When you see passengers walking away from a burning aircraft towing their wheeled carry-on luggage you realise that there is another thing that doesn't seem to be working.

There has been a spate of successful emergency evacuations (San Francisco, Las Vegas and Dubai) from which we have discovered that passengers WILL take their cabin bags during an evacuation, no matter their race or culture.

Locking the overhead bins will only delay their egress as they try to open the lockers. We have to stop complaining about passengers and fix the problem by allowing only small cabin bags on board; a radical change for all players.

This raises another issue: where is each passenger going to place the five lithium batteries they currently bring on board? Their watch, phone, tablet, camera and laptop have to go somewhere. We need to be able to get at each item in-flight when it catches fire. Every passenger needs their medications, documentation, money, and for some cultures … their gold.

13. ICAO Elite Crash Investigators

A US$1 levee on every IATA ticket sold would raise US$3.6 billion a year, every year, to fund air crash investigations.

ICAO should provide a flying-squad of investigators, drawn from member countries, who become the lead investigators in all crashes – providing a repeatable standard of investigation regardless of the country of registration of the aircraft, or where the crash occurs. The best investigators should be chosen to work specifically for ICAO, with the local investigators providing assistance.

It is imperative we resume the search and find the wreckage of MH370. After developing and refining the technology, amassing the equipment and training the crews, we now have an efficient machine that works. To stop them now is like stopping the Olympic marathon just as the competitors are about to enter the stadium. As a species, we are better than that.
Send the searchers back out to investigate the 25,000 square kilometer area at the intersection of the 7th arc and 35 degrees south.
Finding the cause of the crash of MH370 may be crucial for the future of aviation and may even be invaluable on, say, the mission to Mars.

When I think of Captain Zaharie Shah and First Officer Fariq Hamid I see them as real heroes, using every ounce of their skills, knowledge and experience; fighting until their last breath to get their passengers and crew safely on the ground.
Not as terrorists, or pirates … *or idiots.*
They earned their seats in this huge jet.
Until we learn otherwise, let's treat them with the respect they deserve.

RECAPPING

- The Smoke, Fire & Fumes and Smoke Removal checklists need revamping.
- We should remove smoke first and reinstate systems later, after successful system testing.
- Cameras and lights in cabins, cargo and avionics compartments.
- And in landing gear and wheel wells, too.
- Focused, with lights, on the wing's "representative surface" for cold weather operations.
- We need a cockpit indicator, which shows the product of each side of the air-conditioning system, with a smoke sensor.
- Auto cargo fire suppression systems, one for the front and one for the back.
- With a pet-safe compartment.
- Real-time latitude/longitude feedback with monitored engines.
- Real-time asset tracking systems for all long-range aircraft.
- Ejectable black boxes on all new aircraft.
- Modernize the black boxes, making them

pressure-sensitive units that wait, if submerged in deep water, until rescuers arrive before issuing louder pings, with a burst of high-speed Morse that identifies the unique recorder.

- Redesign cockpit oxygen masks; current designs are 25 years old.
- If it is proven that MH370 was crashed due to lithium battery fire, then ban their carriage.
- Passenger's carry-on baggage needs to be miniaturized since we know that they will retrieve them in an emergency.
- We need to send the searchers back out to finish the last 25,000 square kilometers.
- IATA members should collect USD $1 from the sale of each ticket to be used to fund crash investigation 3.6 billion dollars will be collected annually.
- ICAO should run investigation worldwide, drawing the best investigators from their member countries to provide a repeatable standard. Local investigators to assist.

WHAT'S NEXT?

The decision to suspend the search for MH370 can only be political. If you believe that the search should be resumed, feel free to contact your political leaders and request that they continue the search, sending the searchers to the 25,000 square kilometer location at the 7th arc and 35 degrees south.

If you have enjoyed this book I would be grateful if you would go to Amazon's page and post an honest review, or tell a friend.

An author's life is a solitary one, tapping keys in the silence of your office. Reviews on the Amazon site are the reward for all the work. The more reviews from locations all around the world, the more people will buy the book. It's that simple. It's the new word-of-mouth. It's what authors live for.

My dream is to get onto the best-seller lists which can help a book to "breakout" from the masses and gain real attention. Your quick book review will really help me.

If you would like to recommend it on your social media, that'd be great too.

I really value your feedback, please email me at:
contact@thecrashofmh370.com
Whilst I may not be able to reply personally, I promise to read every message. I will reply by tweets to enable all readers to benefit from our conversation.

Thanks once again, now let's get the search resumed as soon as possible.

James.

Website:	www.TheCrashOfMH370.com
Twitter :	TheCrashOfMH370 @MH370crash
Facebook :	The Crash Of MH370 Book
Publishers:	Paperback rights are still available in some markets.
Speaking:	The author is available for speaking engagements, and travels from Melbourne, Australia. Contact Kerryn@CrammondMedia.com

ACKNOWLEDGEMENTS

Mike Exner has been invaluable in correcting the text and helping me understand MH370's initial diversion turn.

An engineer (electrical), entrepreneur and pilot for 50 years, Mike has about 1500 hours in sailplanes and 1500 hours in small airplanes. He was a founding member of Duncan Steel's Independent Group and has been the main IG liaison with ATSB and NTSB; drawing on his atmospheric science, piloting and satellite communications experience to help the IG and ATSB.

(in alphabetical order)

Paul Carruthers - A380 Captain

Geoff Dempster - 777 Captain

Gilles Diharce - Air Traffic Controller, French Ministry of Defense

Mike Exner - Radar Analysis

Michael Jones - Social Media Promotion

Olwyn Jones - Copy Editor / Proofreader / Cover Words

Will Lanting - Boeing Engineer
Caroline LeCann - 777 Captain
Nikki Liddell - Proofreader
Emma Lowans - 777 Captain
Kamma Lyhne - 777 Captain
Geoff Neate - 727 Captain, 767, 737, F28 FO,
                Director Flight Operations
Ro Nixon - Inspiration / Proofreader
Ginny Nixon - Proofreader
Marcus Noonan - Proofreader
Victor Pody - Aviation Photography
Grace Pundyk - Editor / Motivator
Bruce Saunders - Captain Boeing 787 / Airbus
                Acceptance Test Pilot, A320 A330
                Examiner / Boeing 727, 757-767
Derek Scales - Proofreader
Navjot Singh - Proofreader
Chris Sotiropoulos - Legal Counsel
Jon Stikman - Cover Design
Luis Tellez - Promotional Photography
Kerryn Warner - Executive Assistant
Terry Worth - Cover - casting vote
(Name Withheld) - Airbus A380 Test Pilot

ADDITIONAL READING / VIEWING

Brazilian pilot enters 777 Main Equipment Center in-flight

Against all rules about entering an avionics compartment in-flight, a Brazilian pilot shows off the 777 main equipment center.

Jones, Jack. "777 E/E Bay" Video (7'45"). Mar 18,2014.

https://www.youtube.com/watch?v=2S-Cggs1jOo

777 Windscreen Fire Reference

Mick Gilbert made reference to cockpit window fires, this is the accident to which he refers.

Hradecky, Simon. "Accident: Egyptair B772 at Cairo on Jul 29th 2011, cockpit fire" *The Aviation Herald.* Updated Jul 30th 2011.

http://avherald.com/h?article=44078aa7

APPENDIX

Esstrack
www.esstrack.com

Statement from Esstrack CEO Lorne Cole:

"Esstrack has been developing satellite-based aircraft tracking and communication solutions for over five years in support of long distance, overwater, air ambulance operations. Following the disappearance of MH370, commercialisation of the product, and further development of a 'tamper proof' power supply was deemed to be justified.

A fully autonomous system, capable of securely retrieving, analysing, transmitting and storing vital aircraft flight data via various satellite and terrestrial links ensures that operators, regulators, and manufacturers have almost real-time access to important flight parameters and information for operational analysis, or incident and accident investigation. The innovation inherent in this design is the first major step forward since David Warren's 1953 invention of the 'black box' flight data recorder."

LIST OF ABBREVIATIONS

3-F1 The name of one of Inmarsat's satellites
9M-MRO Registration Markings of the aircraft
A-TACS™ Aviation Telecommunications & Communications System (owned by Esstrack)
ACARS Aircraft Communications Addressing and Reporting System A datalink communication system between the airline and the aircraft, transferring messages to the pilot and automatic data to the engineering department. Usually using VHF communication until out of sight or an aerial, then via High Frequency radio or Satellite link.
ADS-B Automatic Dependent Surveillance – Broadcast
ADS-C Automatic Dependent Surveillance – Contract
AMSA Australian Maritime Safety Authority
APASA Asia-Pacific Applied Science Associates
APU Auxiliary Power Unit
ARCC Aeronautical Rescue Coordination Centre
ATC Air Traffic Control(ler)
ATSB Australian Transport Safety Bureau
BA British Airways
BAE British AErospace sometimes written BAe

BBC British Broadcasting Corporation
BFO Burst Frequency Offset
BOM Bureau of Meteorology (Australia)
CASA Civil Aviation Safety Authority
Cb Cumulo Nimbus (thunderstorm) - a type of cloud
CCTV Closed-Circuit TeleVision
CNN Cable News Network media organization (USA)
CPDLC Controller–Pilot Data Link Communications A type of communication between ATC and aircraft using screens and short written messages
CRM Crew Resource Management
CSIRO Commonwealth Scientific and Industrial Research Organisation (Australia)
DCA Department of Civil Aviation (Malaysia)
DETRESFA Distress Phase
Direct to (If issued by ATC) an instruction: "TRACK direct to…"
E2 The name of one of Telesat Anik's satellites
ER extended range
EROS® A brand of quick-donning oxygen mask
ETOPS Extended-range Twin-engine Operational Performance Standards
FAA Federal Aviation Administration
FBI Federal Bureau Of Investigation
FIA International Automobile Federation
FIR Flight Information Region
FL Flight Level (feet above sea level in the

standard atmosphere, QNH 1013mb, divided by ten)
FO First Officer
FSX Microsoft Flight Simulator
GCAA General Civil Aviation Authority (UAE)
GEMS Global Environmental Modelling Systems
GMT Greenwich Mean Time
HCMC Ho Chi Minh City (previously Saigon)
Heathrow Heathrow airport - London (LHR / EGLL)
IATA International Air Transport Association
ICAO International Civil Aviation Organization
IFE In-Flight Entertainment system
IG Duncan Steel's Independent Group.
IOR Indian Ocean Region
ITCZ Inter Tropical Convergence Zone
JFK (KJFK) John Fitzgerald Kennedy airport, New York
KG kilograms
KL Kuala Lumpur
KLIA Kuala Lumpur International Airport
Kts Knots (1 nautical mile in 1 hour = 1 knot = 1.852 kph = 1.15078 mph)
lbs Pounds
LHR London Heathrow airport
LOC-I Loss Of Control In-flight
m meter
MAS Malaysian Airlines
MH Airline Identifier for Malaysian Airlines
MH370 An abbreviation of the flight number

Malaysian Airlines flight 370
Mode S transponder
MOT Ministry of Transport (Malaysia)
NASA National Aeronautics & Space Administration (USA)
Nm Nautical Miles
NOTOC Notification To Captain form submitted to the Captain before departure, detailing special loads and dangerous goods
NTSB National Transport Safety Board
OPCW Organization for the Prohibition of Chemical Weapons
PA Public Address
RAT Ram Air Turbine
RFFS Rescue Fire Fighting Services
Runway 32 Right A runway is named by its direction in degrees magnetic, rounded to the nearest five degrees and divided by ten. 321 degrees becomes 320 / 10 = Runway 32 If there are multiple runways they become L = Left, C=Center, R = Right. Before takeoff pilots glance at the runway number and check it against the magnetic compass, to ensure the compass is operating correctly.
RVSM Reduced Vertical Separation Minima
SAS Special Air Service
SATCOM Satellite Telephone Communications system
SMS Short Message Service
SOS Save Our Souls (superseded by MAYDAY,

MAYDAY, MAYDAY distress message)
Squawk Code A four-digit number issued by ATC and placed by the pilots into the transponder. That number is captured by radar and displayed on the ATC radar screen. Once the pilot says his number, or replies by pressing an ident button on the transponder, the ATC identifies the aircraft. Under radar identification ATC can apply tighter separation standards.
SSR Secondary Surveillance Radar
TAC Thrust Asymmetry Compensation
TCAS Traffic Collision Avoidance System
TRE Type Rating Examiner
TRI Type Rating Instructor
UAE United Arab Emirates
UK United Kingdom
ULD Unit Load Device
UPS United Parcel Service
US United States of America
USA United States of America
UTC Universal Time Coordinated (previously Greenwich Mean Time)
VHF Very High Frequency The primary type of radio system used by ATC and aircraft, propagation is line-of-sight
VIP Very Important Person

GLOSSARY OF TERMS

Edited glossary from the Malaysian investigator's report "Factual Information: Safety Investigation of MH370".

When the following terms are used, they have the following meaning:

Aircraft - Any machine that can give derive support in the atmosphere from the reactions of the air other than the reactions of the air against the earth's surface.

Alert Phase - A situation wherein apprehension exists as to the safety of an aircraft or marine vessel, and of the persons on board.

Alerting Post - Any facility intended to serve as an intermediary between a person reporting an emergency and a rescue co-ordination centre or rescue sub-centre.

Blind transmission - A transmission from one station to another station in circumstances where two-way communication cannot be established but where it is believed that the called station is able to receive the transmission.

Cabin Crew Member - A crew member who performs, in the interest of safety passengers, duties assigned by the operator or the pilot-in-command of the aircraft, but who shall not act as a flight crew member.

Cargo - Any property carried on an aircraft other than mail, stores and accompanied or mishandled baggage.

Causes - Actions, omissions, events, conditioning, or a combination of thereof, which led to the accident or incident. The identification of causes does not imply the assignment of fault or the determination of administrative, civil or criminal liability.

Co-ordinated Universal Time (UTC) - International term for time at the prime meridian.

Conversion Training - Training required when a pilot is posted to a different aircraft type or model.

Detresfa - The code word used to designate a distress phase.

Distress Phase - A situation wherein there is reasonable certainty than an aircraft and its occupants are threatened by grave and imminent danger or require immediate assistance.

Emergency Phase - A generic term meaning, as the case may be, uncertainty phase, or distress phase.

Filed Flight Plan - The flight plan as filed with an ATS unit by the pilot or a designated representative, without any subsequent changes.

Flight plan - Specified information provided to

the air traffic units, relative to an intended flight or portion of a flight of an aircraft.

Flight Recorder - Any type of recorder installed in the aircraft for the purpose of complementing accident/incident investigation - Annex 6, Parts I, II and III, for specifications relating to flight recorders.

Incident - An occurrence, other than an accident, associated with the operation of an aircraft which affects or could affect the safety operation - The types of incidents which are of main interest to the International Civil Aviation Organization for accident prevention studies are listed in Attachment C of Annex 13.

Inmarsat - A system of geostationary satellites for world-wide mobile communications services, and which support the Global Maritime Distress and Safety System and other emergency communications systems.

Investigation - A process conducted for the purpose of accident prevention which includes the gathering and analysis of information, the drawing of conclusions, including the determination of causes and/or contributing factors and, when appropriate, the making of safety recommendations.

NOTAM - A notice distributed by means of telecommunication containing information concerning the establishment, condition of change in any aeronautical facility, service, procedure or hazard, the timely knowledge of which is essential to personnel concerned with flight operations.

Operator - A person, organization or enterprise engaged in or offering to engage in an aircraft operation.

Pilot-in-command - The pilot responsible for the operation and the safety of the aircraft during flight time.

Safety Recommendation - A proposal of an accident investigation authority based on information derived from an investigation, made with the intention or preventing accidents or incidents and which in no case has the purpose of creating a presumption of blame or liability for an accident or incident. In addition to safety recommendations arising from accident and incident investigations, safety recommendations may result from the diverse sources, including safety studies.

State of Design - The State having jurisdiction over the organization responsible for the type design.

State of Manufacture - The State having jurisdiction over the organization responsible for the final assembly of the aircraft.

State of Occurrence - The State in the territory of which an accident or incident occurs.

State of the Operator - The State in which the operator's principal place of business is located or, if there is no such place of business, the operator's permanent residence.

State of Registry - The State on whose register the aircraft is entered. In the case of the registration of aircraft of an international operating agency on other than a national basis, the States constituting the agency are jointly and severally bound to assume the obligations which, under the Chicago Convention, attach to a State of Registry. See, in this regard, the Council Resolution of 14 December 1967 on Nationality and Registration of Aircraft Operated by International Operating Agencies which can be found in Policy and Guidance Material on the Economic Regulation of International Air Transport (Doc 9587).

Knot (kt) - A unit of speed equal to one nautical mile per hour.

Pilot-in-Command - The pilot responsible for the operation and the safety of the aircraft

during flight time.

Uncertainty Phase - A situation wherein doubt exists as to the safety of an aircraft or marine vessel, and of the persons on board.

www.**TheCrashOfMH370**.com

The website of the book includes:

Maps of the flight

Mike McKay's Letter
& Location of Oil Rig

Photo of the aircraft

Photo of the Straits Of Malacca
where the plane was last recorded on radar

Photo of the KLIA Security
Checkpoint

Photo of the border between India
and Pakistan

Photo and video of an inflight
interception of a Jet Airways 777

… and more

www.**TheCrashOfMH370**.com

Also by James Nixon:

SLEEPING FOR PILOTS
& CABIN CREW
(And Other Insomiacs)
by
The Anonymous
Airbus A380 Captain*

The book that lifts the sheets on how to sleep whenever YOU want.

This book consists of everything I have learnt about sleeping. Getting control of your sleep is the only way new aircrew can turn this job into a long-term career.

Divided this book into two parts, the first is an analysis of the 20 variables that can affect your sleep. The second half is the 'how-to' section. Tips and tricks tested in the laboratory of life, the harshest conditions in the world: the *moving sleep cycle* of the international flight crew.

Like no-one else does it.

Fire fighters, police, doctors, nurses, shift workers all get a roster that allows a sign-on at the same time for up to six days in a row. They feel like crap, but they can get a routine going. As aircrew, we rise with the sun, fly to a location, arrive in the late afternoon, have twenty-two hours off then fly back all night, arriving before the sun rises on day three. On day four we sign-on in the afternoon and fly until midnight. And so on. If we are travelling east and west then jet lag adds to the mix.

There are entire industries trying to sell us things to sleep faster, better, easier, softer and longer. Few of them work. Some are outright dangerous and can put our flight crew licenses at risk, not to mention the lives of our passengers.

For a year I trawled through hundreds of websites and research papers to support the suggestions I offer. Each one is listed in the footnotes so readers can check the latest information.

This is the book **you** would have written if you had interviewed a few thirty-year veterans and spent about a year of your days-off trolling through the published research papers, newspaper and magazine stories and websites.

I have tried to distill some heavy topics into light reading; and can guarantee that if the reader does everything I suggest, they will get control of their sleep; sleeping better than they've ever slept before.

To reinforce points, I have included "From The Logbook" sections which give amusing anecdotes. Feedback is that readers love these insights.

The section on Stress Management caused the book to become a Kindle Bestseller.

Go to Amazon, search Sleeping Pilots, or click

http://tinyurl.com/SleepingForPilots

or visit
www.ProfessionalSleeping.com

* When I wrote the book my employment contract precluded writing a book under my own name.

SLEEPING FOR PILOTS & CABIN CREW
(And Other Insomiacs)

Reader Reviews

Essential Reading For Aircrew
(& anyone else working
the backside of the clock)

'I gave up a career that I loved, in large part because the night shifts, and subsequent fatigue, were killing me. Had this informative, well researched, and humorous book been available, I might still be flying.'
IH, (former) A380 Captain

***

'Trying to study for the simulator but
made the fatal mistake of uploading
"Sleeping For Pilots & Cabin Crew"
onto my kindle!

I cannot put it down and laughing
out loud at some anecdotes.

Every shift worker needs this book!'
' ... as entertaining as Bill Bryson's
books I reckon! '

CJ, Boeing 777 Captain

***

ENDNOTES

The following pages list all the end notes in order.

Hyperlinks have been removed for the paperback version of the book.

The kindle eBook, available at Amazon.com (search MH370), contains all live hyperlinks.

1 **Automatic Dependent Surveillance-Broadcast (ADS-B)** – Wikipedia.
A surveillance technology in which an aircraft determines its position via satellite navigation and periodically broadcasts it, enabling it to be tracked.

https://en.wikipedia.org/wiki/Automatic_dependent_surveillance_%E2%80%93_broadcast

2 **Michael McKay's email**
Ohlheiser, Abby. "Oil Rig Worker Thinks He Saw Malaysia Air Flight 370 Go Down in Flames." *The Atlantic*. March 12, 2014.

http://www.theatlantic.com/international/archive/2014/03/oil-rig-worker-says-he-saw-malaysia-air-flight-370-go-down/359093/

3 **Investigator's Factual Information Report**
Government of Malaysia. Ministry of Transport Malaysia Safety Investigation Team for MH370. "Factual Information: Safety Investigation of MH370." Putrajaya: Govt. Malaysia. April 15, 2015 (updated).

http://mh370.mot.gov.my/download/FactualInformation.pdf

4 **ATSB Reports Page**
Australian Transport Safety Board, The search for MH370, Updates, Reports, December 20, 2016.

https://www.atsb.gov.au/mh370-pages/updates/reports/

5 **Michael McKay's email**
Ohlheiser, Abby. "Oil Rig Worker Thinks He Saw Malaysia Air Flight 370 Go Down in Flames." *The Atlantic.* March 12, 2014.

http://www.theatlantic.com/international/archive/2014/03/oil-rig-worker-says-he-saw-malaysia-air-flight-370-go-down/359093/

6 **International Civil Aviation Organization (ICAO)**
http://www.iata.org/about/Pages/index.aspx

7 **International Air Transport Association (IATA)**
http://www.iata.org/

8 **Examples where NTSB has asked the FAA to address issues**

"The National Transportation Safety Board said that poor design, manufacturing and testing caused the fire in the lithium-ion battery—deficiencies it blamed on Boeing and one of its suppliers. The board also faulted the FAA for failing to identify the design defects."
Petersen, Melody. **"Probe blames Boeing and FAA for 787 Dreamliner battery fire."** *LA Times.* Dec 1, 2014.

http://www.latimes.com/business/la-fi-boeing-dreamliner-20141202-story.html

Wald, Matthew L. **"Safety Board Determines Pilot Fatigue Caused Skid."** *New York Times.* June 11, 2008.

http://www.nytimes.com/2008/06/11/business/11pilots.html?partner=rssnyt&emc=rss

Grady, Mary. **"NTSB Blames FAA in Pilot's Death."** AVWeb.

http://www.avweb.com/avwebflash/news/NTSBBlamesFAAInPilotsDeath_198998-1.html?CMP=OTC-RSS

9 MH370 Official Website
The Malaysian Ministry of Transport is the lead investigator.

http://www.mh370.gov.my/index.php/en/

10 Department Of Civil Aviation – Malaysia (DCA)
http://www.dca.gov.my/

11 Malaysia Airline (MS)
The airline was known as Malaysian Airlines (MAS) at the time of the crash. Subsequently, the private shareholders have been paid out, the government has taken control of the airline, de-listed from the stock exchange and changed its name to Malaysia Airlines (MS).
www.malaysiaairlines.com

12 Civil Aviation Safety Authority (CASA)
www.casa.gov.au

13 Airservices
www.airservicesaustralia.com

14 Australian Transport Safety Bureau (ATSB)
http://www.atsb.gov.au/about_atsb/overview/

15 **Australian Maritime Safety Authority (AMSA)**
http://www.amsa.gov.au/search-and-rescue/

16 **AMSA Bombardier Challenger CL-604 special mission jets**

http://www.amsa.gov.au/search-and-rescue/amsas-role-in-search-and-rescue/challenger/index.html

17 **ATSB leads underwater search operations for the missing aircraft.**
ATSB, "Inaccuracies in reporting on the search for MH370" - January, 18 2016.

https://www.atsb.gov.au/newsroom/correcting-records/inaccuracies-in-reporting-on-the-search-for-mh370/

18 **ATSB Report - Definition Of Underwater Search Areas**
"MH370 - Definition of Underwater Search Areas" - Introduction page 1, ATSB Transport Safety Report, External Aviation Investigation AE-2014-054 26 June 2014 (updated 18 August 2014).

https://www.atsb.gov.au/media/5243942/ae-2014-054_mh370_-_definition_of_underwater_search_areas_18aug2014.pdf

19 **ATSB MH370 Reports page**
http://www.atsb.gov.au/mh370-pages/updates/reports/

20 Captain Shah was uncle of Anwar Ibrahim's daughter-in-law
Webmaster, M T. "Anwar says Capt Zaharie related to his daughter-in-law"
Malaysia Today. March 18, 2014.

http://www.malaysia-today.net/anwar-says-capt-zaharie-related-to-his-daughter-in-law/

21 Captain Shah's brother in law, Asuad Khan, interviewed.
Wockner, Cindy. "Missing Malaysia Airlines flight MH370 pilot Captain Zaharie Ahmad Shah not to blame for disappearance, family insist"
News Corp Australia. June 16, 2014.

http://www.news.com.au/world/missing-malaysia-airlines-flight-mh370-pilot-captain-zaharie-ahmad-shah-not-to-blame-for-disappearance-family-insist/news-story/0c113697df7b24b040fe54fb572de1f5

22 Captain Shah's home simulator (video)

https://www.youtube.com/watch?v=YRt2QIBho4w

23 Flight Simulator #9
Top 10 gaming programs sold in 2007.
Gillen, Kieron."News Just In: World of Warcraft Sells Many Copies"
Rock Paper Shotgun. January 28th, 2008.

https://www.rockpapershotgun.com/tag/sales-figures/

24 Microsoft Flight Simulator - 21 million copies sold by June 1999

Grupping, Jos. "The Story of Flight Simulator" *Flight Simulator History.* March 04, 2005.

http://fshistory.simflight.com/fsh/versions.htm

25 Microsoft Flight Simulator demonstration (video)

https://www.youtube.com/watch?v=4vD1B4yOsK4

26 Flight Simulator Multiplayer Live website

http://www.fsxmultiplayer.com/sessions.php

27 Captain Shah's brother in law, Asuad Khan, interviewed

Wockner, Cindy. "Missing Malaysia Airlines flight MH370 pilot Captain Zaharie Ahmad Shah not to blame for disappearance, family insist" *News Corp Australia.* June 16, 2014.

http://www.news.com.au/world/missing-malaysia-airlines-flight-mh370-pilot-captain-zaharie-ahmad-shah-not-to-blame-for-disappearance-family-insist/news-story/0c113697df7b24b040fe54fb572de1f5

28 Air Traffic Control exchanges with MH370

Government of Malaysia. Ministry of Transport Malaysia Safety Investigation Team for MH370. "Factual Information: Safety Investigation of MH370." Putrajaya: Govt. Malaysia. April 15, 2015 (updated) page 259 Appendix 1.18E page 19/29.

http://mh370.mot.gov.my/download/FactualInformation.pdf

29 **Exchanges between Air Traffic Control and MAS OPS**
Government of Malaysia. Ministry of Transport Malaysia Safety Investigation Team for MH370. "Factual Information: Safety Investigation of MH370." Putrajaya: Govt. Malaysia. April 15, 2015 (updated) page 272 Appendix 1.18F page 3/125.

http://mh370.mot.gov.my/download/FactualInformation.pdf

30 **The book on the search by Australia's investigators from the Defence Science & Technology Group, in South Australia.**
Davey, Sam, Neil Gordon, Ian Holland, Mark Rutten, and Jason Williams. *"Bayesian Methods in the Search for MH370."* Singapore: Springer, 2016.

http://link.springer.com/book/10.1007/978-981-10-0379-0

31 **Solar storms can damage satellites**
Odenwald, Sten. " They Call Them 'Satellite Anomalies' ". *The 23rd Cycle: Learning to Live with a Stormy Star.* New York: Columbia University Press, 2001.
Accessed author's website

http://www.solarstorms.org/SWChapter6.pdf

32 **Space Weather**
Kennewell, John and McDonald, Andrew. "Satellite Communications and Space Weather."
Australian Government - *Bureau of Meteorology.* Undated.

http://www.sws.bom.gov.au/Educational/1/3/2

33 Details on the 1,419 satellites currently orbiting Earth

Union of Concerned Scientists Satellite Database - August 11, 2016.

http://www.ucsusa.org/nuclear-weapons/space-weapons/satellite-database#.WJmSoxJ962w

34 Inmarsat-3F1's position during MH370's flight

Steel, Duncan. "The locations of Inmarsat-3F1 during the flight of MH370" - March 18, 2015.

http://www.duncansteel.com/archives/category/mh370/page/11

Steel is part of the "Independent Group (IG)":
"The IG is a worldwide group of unaffiliated individuals with diverse backgrounds and skills who coalesced in the months following the MH370 disappearance to discuss, using an on-line mailing list, the technical aspects of the incident with a view towards assisting, through public disclosure of studies, the process of selection of priority search areas. Our focus has been on the recovery of the aircraft, so that forensic analysis can be performed to determine the root cause of this tragedy."

The IG determined the location of MH370 and issued a press release.
"Searching for MH370 airliner in the wrong place." September 30th, 2014

http://thehuntformh370.info/content/searching-mh370-airliner-wrong-place

35 Dr. David Griffin of CSIRO – Drift Analysis

Griffin, David. "MH370 – Drift Analysis" - Updated January 21, 2017.
Articles detailing the research done and the Global Drifter Program.

http://www.marine.csiro.au/~griffin/MH370/

36 Bob McDonald's CBC Radio interview with Dr. David Griffin

McDonald, Bob. "Was the search for Malaysia Airlines flight 370 called off too soon?" CBC Radio Quirks & Quarks - January, 21, 2017.

http://www.cbc.ca/radio/quirks/antarctic-evacuation-sloppy-science-laser-mice-and-more-1.3942939/was-the-search-for-malaysia-airlines-flight-370-called-off-too-soon-1.3945085

37 ATSB - **"CSIRO Drift Report 2"** - 13th April 2017.

http://www.atsb.gov.au/publications/investigation_reports/2014/aair/ae-2014-054/

38 Richard Godfrey – Goose Barnacles

Independent researcher Richard Godfrey has written a compelling article about goose barnacles, as found on MH370's recovered flaperon. He is part of the Independent Group (IG)
Godfrey, Richard. "The long hunt for a diversion airport - Goose Barnacles." October 18th, 2016.

http://www.duncansteel.com/archives/category/mh370

39 **Official report Space Shuttle Challenger crash**
"Report of the Presidential Commission on the Space Shuttle Challenger Accident." June 6th, 1986.

http://history.nasa.gov/rogersrep/genindex.htm

40 **Space Shuttle Challenger disaster**– Wikipedia
"Recovery of debris. The crew cabin was severely crushed and fragmented from the extreme impact forces; one member of the search team described it as "largely a pile of rubble with wires protruding from it"."

https://en.wikipedia.org/wiki/Space_Shuttle_Challenger_disaster

41 **The crash of Swissair Flight 111** – Wikipedia

https://en.wikipedia.org/wiki/Swissair_Flight_111

The jet disintegrated into more than million pieces
"It is estimated that more than 2 million pieces of wreckage were recovered. To organize the storage of this debris, a grid system was laid out in "A" Hangar to represent various sections of the aircraft …"
Transportation Safety Board of Canada. "Aviation Investigation Report A98H0003 - Recovery Procedures." Updated April 24, 2013.

http://www.tsb.gc.ca/eng/rapports-reports/aviation/1998/a98h0003/02sti/16researchandinvestigation/testsandresearch.asp#recoveryprocedures

42 The results of the search
"MH370 - First Principals Review" Report. ATSB – December 20, 2016

https://www.atsb.gov.au/media/5772107/ae2014054_final-first-principles-report.pdf

43 Jeff Wise - President Putin stole the 777
Wise, Jeff. "New York: How Crazy Am I to Think I Actually Know Where That Malaysia Airlines Plane Is?" Jeff Wise. March 7, 2015.

http://jeffwise.net/2015/03/07/new-york-how-crazy-am-i-to-think-i-actually-know-where-that-malaysia-airlines-plane-is/

44 Keith Ledgerwood - In Singapore's shadow
Ledgerwood, Keith. "Did Malaysian Airlines 370 disappear using SIA68/SQ68 (another 777)?" Keith Ledgerwood. March 17, 2014.

http://keithledgerwood.com/post/79838944823/did-malaysian-airlines-370-disappear-using

45 *777 Rapid Descent (video)*
Watch Flight.org's Captain Ken Pascoe perform a rapid descent due to a cabin pressure problem in a 777 simulator.

https://www.youtube.com/watch?v=4EaQLca9rJY

46 Fox News Conspiracy Theory (video)
Fox News' Retired US Air Force Lt. General Thomas Mc.Inerney believed that Pakistan wanted to steal a Malaysian 777.

https://www.youtube.com/watch?v=UWiVkShm8cw

47 **Affects of Hypoxia On Aircrew (video)**
During an altitude chamber training, a candidate displayed symptoms of hypoxia, after exceeding his "time of useful consciousness".
Cummings, Christopher. "Hypoxia - 4 of spades" Video (3'31"). September 2, 2011.

https://www.youtube.com/watch?v=UN3W4d-5RPo

48 **Helios Airways Crash** – Wikipedia
Helios Airways Flight 522. A lack of oxygen incapacitated the crew.

https://en.wikipedia.org/wiki/Helios_Airways_Flight_522

49 **Image of a deployed "rubber jungle"**
Mikka H. "Oxygen masks in airplane bathrooms: Terrorism risk?" Photograph.
The Week. March 11, 2011.

http://theweek.com/articles/486464/oxygen-masks-airplane-bathrooms-terrorism-risk

50 **Air Traffic Control exchanges with MH370**
Government of Malaysia. Ministry of Transport Malaysia Safety Investigation Team for MH370. "Factual Information: Safety Investigation of MH370." Putrajaya: Govt. Malaysia. April 15, 2015 (updated) page 259 Appendix 1.18E page 19/29.

http://mh370.mot.gov.my/download/FactualInformation.pdf

51 **Definition of severe turbulence**
"Turbulence that causes large, abrupt changes in altitude and/or attitude. It usually causes large

variations in indicated airspeed. Aircraft maybe momentarily out of control."
"Light, Moderate or Severe Turbulence ... How Are They Defined?" Citizen Sailor. August 30th, 2009

http://www.navyaircrew.com/blog/2009/08/30/light-moderate-or-severe-turbulencehow-are-they-defined/

52 Germanwings Flight 9525 – Wikipedia
The crash of an A320 was deliberately caused by the co-pilot, Andreas Lubitz, who had previously been treated for suicidal tendencies and declared "unfit to work" by a doctor.

https://en.wikipedia.org/wiki/Germanwings_Flight_9525

53 Psychological screening for pilots
de Castella, Tom. "How are pilots psychologically screened?" BBC News Magazine. March 27, 2015.

http://www.bbc.com/news/magazine-32075809

54 ETOPS – Wikipedia
Extended-range Twin-engine Operational Performance Standards (ETOPS) Explained

https://en.wikipedia.org/wiki/ETOPS

55 British Airways Flight 38 – Wikipedia
A British Airways 777 crashed short of the runway at Heathrow due to double engine failure.

https://en.wikipedia.org/wiki/British_Airways_Flight_38

56 Mick Gilbert's paper regarding multiple failures

Gilbert, Mick. "An Analysis of MH370's Flight Path Between Waypoint IGARI and the top of the Malacca Strait, a Review of Potential Vulnerabilities Specific to Airplane 9M-MRO and a Hypothesis Regarding Possible In Flight Events and an End-of-Flight Scenario"
Mick Gilbert V3.11 December 21, 2016

https://www.dropbox.com/s/lf0f61mzkt3rug3/MH370%20Research%20V3.11.pdf

57 Professor James Reason's Swiss Cheese Plane Crashes – Wikipedia

https://en.wikipedia.org/wiki/Swiss_cheese_model

58 United Parcel Service (UPS) Flight 6

United Arab Emirates Government. UAE General Civil Aviation Authority Air Accident Investigation Sector. "Final Air Accident Investigation Report: Uncontained Cargo Fire Leading to Loss of Control Inflight and Uncontrolled Descent Into Terrain." Abu Dhabi: UAE Govt. 2010. Pages 121-124 (lithium batteries).

https://www.gcaa.gov.ae/en/ePublication/admin/iradmin/Lists/Incidents%20Investigation%20Reports/Attachments/40/2010-2010%20-%20Final%20Report%20-%20Boeing%20747-44AF%20-%20N571UP%20-%20Report%2013%202010.pdf

59 Lithium Battery Packaging

Government of Malaysia. Ministry of Transport Malaysia Safety Investigation Team for MH370.

"Factual Information: Safety Investigation of MH370." Putrajaya: Govt. Malaysia. April 15, 2015 (updated).p106 Figures 1.18G & 1.18H - Packing of Batteries by Motorola Solutions

http://mh370.mot.gov.my/download/FactualInformation.pdf

60 Lithium battery fire aircrew training videos
FAA Training Video
Advanced Imaging, Operations Planning, FAA Air Traffic Organization.
"Extinguishing In-Flight Laptop Computer Fires." (video 10'40") October 2007.

https://www.youtube.com/watch?v=vS6KA_Si-m8

"Aircare FireSock™" (Video 3'30")
FireSock™ is a trademark of Aircare Solutions Group. January 9, 2013.

https://www.youtube.com/watch?v=aE5M7xM40Ak

61 Chris Goodfellow's theory.
Zurcher, Anthony. "An MH370 theory that was simple, compelling and wrong." Echo Chambers, BBC News. March 19, 2014.

http://www.bbc.com/news/blogs-echochambers-26640114

62 Before you contact me, I wrote *"airborne wing fire"*. In June 2016, a 777, "SQ 368" had an oil leak and returned to land. The engine had not been secured prior to landing and caught fire on the ground, setting fire to the wing.

63 Aerotoxic Association website, one smoke/fumes event every 2,000 flights.

Aerotoxic Association supports those affected by aerotoxic syndrome and keeps a record of smoke / fumes events on their website. They declare that there are 1,300 fume events every day in the UK & USA.

http://aerotoxic.org/

The Aviation Herald

Usually, the first place where we learns of events in the industry is on their website. They list every *major* incident worldwide in real time. Smoke / Fumes events are the most common.

http://avherald.com/

64 ATSB's and CASA's joint report about smoke and fume events.

Australian Transport Safety Bureau & Civil Aviation Safety Authority. "An analysis of fumes and smoke events in Australian aviation 2008-2012" ATSB Transport Safety Report AR-2013-213. May 20, 2014.

https://www.atsb.gov.au/publications/2014/ar-2013-213/

65 Damaged Lithium battery causing fumes (video)

Burn Hard Zen's "Lithium Battery Causing Extreme Fumes When Cut" (3'40")

https://www.youtube.com/watch?v=BLc74Qpvweg

66 UPS 6 Crash - Captain disengages autopilot
United Arab Emirates Government. UAE General Civil Aviation Authority Air Accident Investigation Sector. "Final Air Accident Investigation Report: Uncontained Cargo Fire Leading to Loss of Control Inflight and Uncontrolled Descent Into Terrain." Abu Dhabi: UAE Govt. 2010. Page 24 Captain disengages autopilot.

https://www.gcaa.gov.ae/en/ePublication/admin/iradmin/Lists/Incidents%20Investigation%20Reports/Attachments/40/2010-2010%20-%20Final%20Report%20-%20Boeing%20747-44AF%20-%20N571UP%20-%20Report%2013%202010.pdf

67 Boeing's cargo fire protection systems
Hipsher, Carol & Ferguson, Douglas E. "Fire Protection: cargo compartments"
Boeing *Aeromagazine*. Page 15. Q2, 2011

http://www.boeing.com/commercial/aeromagazine/articles/2011_q2/3/

68 Smoke / Fire / Fumes & Smoke Removal Checklists
Boeing's presentation explaining the design and rationale for each step of the Smoke / Fire / Fumes and Smoke Removal checklists.
McKenzie, Bill. "Smoke/Fire/Fumes Smoke/Fire/Fumes Industry Initiative" 65 slide Powerpoint presentation. Boeing. 2006

http://www.smartcockpit.com/download.php?path=docs/&file=Smoke_Fire_Fume_Initiative.pdf

Delta – 777 Quick Reference Handbook. Revision 15 February 15, 2008
NOTE : NOT FOR OPERATIONAL USE
Smoke / Fire / Fumes checklist page 8.12   Smoke Removal checklist page 8.15

http://www.aviationforall.com/wp-content/uploads/2016/09/Boeing-777-QRH.pdf

69 Hydrogen Cyanide - symptoms
Organization For The Prohibition Of Chemical Weapons (OPCW) lists hydrogen cyanide's symptoms "Hydrogen Cyanide". Undated.

https://www.opcw.org/about-chemical-weapons/types-of-chemical-agent/blood-agents/hydrogen-cyanide/

70 The Station Night Club fire in Rhode Island 2003 – Wikipedia
A fast-moving fire with intense black smoke engulfed the club in 5½ minutes killing 100 people and injuring 230. Another 132 escaped uninjured. (Updated January 27, 2017)

https://en.wikipedia.org/wiki/The_Station_nightclub_fire

71 Dihedral definition – Wikipedia
Dihedral angle is the upward angle from horizontal of the wings or tailplane of a fixed-wing aircraft. Dihedral effect is a critical factor in the stability of an aircraft about the roll axis (the spiral mode).

https://en.wikipedia.org/wiki/Dihedral_(aeronautics)

72 Boeing's end of flight simulations

ATSB "MH370 Search and Debris Examination Update." Transport Safety Report AE-2014-054. End Of Flight Simulations, Page 13. 2nd November 2016

https://www.atsb.gov.au/media/5771939/ae-2014-054_mh370-search-and-debris-update_2nov-2016_v2.pdf

73 Swissair 111 - The longer it takes to complete a prescribed checklist

The longer it takes to complete a prescribed checklist that is designed to de-energize a smoke source, the greater the chance that the smoke source could intensify or become an ignition source and start a fire.

The Transportation Safety Board of Canada (TSB). "In-Flight Fire Leading to Collision with Water. Swissair Transport Limited McDonnell Douglas MD-11 HB-IWF Peggy's Cove, Nova Scotia 5 nm SW - 2 September 1998" Section 1.14.4 "Time Required to Troubleshoot in Odour/Smoke Situations" page 109 Report Number A98H0003. Undated.

http://www.tsb.gc.ca/eng/rapports-reports/aviation/1998/a98h0003/a98h0003.pdf

74 South African Airways crash ZS-SAS recommendation (6)

https://aviation-safety.net/database/record.php?id=19871128-0

Thanks to **Mark Young** for this important fact.

75 **Ejectable Flight Recorder** – Wikipedia
Flight Recorder, Proposed requirements
US Congressman David Price is trying, once again, to launch ejectable flight recorder legislation.

https://en.wikipedia.org/wiki/Flight_recorder

76 **Real-time tracking is coming – IATA**
Kjelgaard, Chris. "Tracking aircraft everywhere is almost within reach" IATA Airlines International Technology / Global. May 31, 2016.

http://airlines.iata.org/analysis/tracking-aircraft-everywhere-is-almost-within-reach

77 **Airservices achieves 14 mins real-time tracking over the Pacific Ocean**
Since June 2015 all flights across the Pacific Ocean between Australia, New Zealand and the United States are being more frequently tracked by air traffic controllers using existing satellite-based communications equipment called Automatic Dependent Surveillance-Contract (ADS-C)
"Oceanic flight tracking" Airservices. July 8, 2016.

http://www.airservicesaustralia.com/services/how-air-traffic-control-works/oceanic-flight-tracking/

78 **ADS-C - definition**
Automatic Dependent Surveillance-Contract (ADS-C) definition and procedures.
International Civil Aviation Organization, "Global Operational Data Link Document (GOLD)" - second edition 26 April 2013, Chapter 2. Overview

of data link operations, 2.2.6 Automatic dependent surveillance – contract (ADS-C)
pages 2-46 — 2.64 (pp 88-101 of 404)

http://www.icao.int/APAC/Documents/edocs/GOLD_2Edition.pdf

79 Skytrac
Skytrac performance trending & quality assurance services. Skytrac Inflight tracks altitude, attitude, speed, fuel consumption and more for better situational awareness, directly communicating in real-time when an aircraft deviates from safe operating parameters.

http://www.skytrac.ca/skytrac-insight/

80 Spidertracks
Spidertracks is a world leader in satellite tracking devices for aircraft. Designed and built in New Zealand, Spiders continue to push the standard of real-time aircraft tracking.

http://www.spidertracks.com/

81 JetCity
JetCity is the one of a handful of Australian air charter companies that owns, operates and maintains its own fleet of distinctive luxury jets and aircraft.

http://www.jetcity.com.au/index.php?pg=501

82 Esstrack

Esstrack manufacturers innovative satellite voice-data-tracking-telemetry communications systems for the aviation, marine, transport & recreational markets.

http://www.esstrack.com/

83 The EROS oxygen mask

"Zodiac Aerospace Eros MC 10 MXP6 Oxygen Mask" Training Video (5'01"). Oct 18,2015

https://www.youtube.com/watch?v=5tkjAB820Pw&t=21s

[**TIP**: To ensure you are receiving 100% oxygen, slide your right hand up the oxygen hose. As you reach the mask your thumb falls naturally on the 100% / Normal switch. Pushing it up, towards your throat gives you 100%.]

www.ingramcontent.com/pod-product-compliance
Lightning Source LLC
Chambersburg PA
CBHW021125300426
44113CB00006B/293